A GREEN
LIGHT
FOR MOM

A GREEN LIGHT FOR MOM

A Boy's Journey through a Deployment

JAYDEN M. SEMOTAN

A GREEN LIGHT FOR MOM
A BOY'S JOURNEY THROUGH A DEPLOYMENT

Illustrations by: Lori Hendrix
> *4402 Stonefield Dr*
> *Oshkosh, WI 54902*
> *920-410-3385*

iUniverse books may be ordered through booksellers or by contacting:

iUniverse
1663 Liberty Drive
Bloomington, IN 47403
www.iuniverse.com
1-800-Authors (1-800-288-4677)

ISBN: 978-1-5320-7178-2 (sc)
ISBN: 978-1-5320-7177-5 (e)

Library of Congress Control Number: 2019904250

Print information available on the last page.

iUniverse rev. date: 04/17/2019

Chapter 1

THE NEWS

On Saturday, April 1, 2017, my life changed. I was told that my mom was going on a deployment. I felt like crying. I was so sad because she would be gone for over six months. The first questions I asked her were:

- Are you going to war?
- Are you going to die?
- Do you get guns?
- When will the deployment start?
- Who will do everything that you do, Mom?

My mom told me that it would be OK and that she was going to support the war. She wouldn't die because she was too smart, and she would have guns if she needed them, so that made me feel better. She told me her deployment would start sometime around January 2018. She also said that she was going to someplace in the Middle East. Lastly, she told me that Dad was going to try to do everything she does, but I had to be a big boy and do some stuff to help, too.

My mom has been in the military my whole life. She is in the 128th Air National Guard in Milwaukee, Wisconsin. It is very similar to the Air Force Reserves. She reports for a Guard weekend once a month and has to do a couple other weeks throughout the year for annual training. Although I am proud of her for doing this, it has made me a bit angry at times because she misses out on so much with our family.

On Monday night, Mom let me know that she had told my school's principal, Mr. Walter, and my teacher, Mrs. Halleen, about the deployment. This made me feel better at first because I figured that if I got sad, they would be there to help me. But the next day, I felt differently. I didn't want my mom to tell anyone else because I wanted it to be our little secret. I felt like if too many people knew, they would start to crowd me. They would come around me and ask me lots of questions that I didn't want to answer. They would also try to make me feel better, which could sometimes get on my nerves. I wanted to deal with this just between my family, my teacher, and my principal. I didn't know how to explain it. I just wanted to be alone and not have to answer a bunch of questions about how I was feeling.

A few days later, I kept thinking about the deployment. When Dad was putting me to bed, I got really close to him and I whispered that I felt like I was going to die. Dad asked me why I would say something like that and I told him that it was because of Mom's deployment. He said, "It's going to be OK." He told me not to worry about it. I asked Dad if Qatar, where Mom would be, was going to war with the United States of America. Dad told me that Qatar is a very friendly country. He said that Mom would be going to a base there to support the war efforts. I asked him why Mom had to do this, and he said it was something that she had to do for the Air Force and for our country. Unfortunately, I continued to feel sad, mad, and very frustrated because it seemed unfair that my mom had to go on this deployment and other people's moms didn't.

Sometime within the next week or two, my mom and dad told me that we were going to go to a counselor to help me get the deployment off my mind. I knew what a counselor was because we had one at our school. The school counselor is a peer counselor, and she mostly talks about respect. She also helps us deal with arguments that happened during recess and in class. Going to a counselor made me feel a little happier because I would get to tell someone about the deployment who wouldn't laugh at me or make me feel like I was wrong for how I was feeling. I worried that if I went to school and told any of my friends about it, they would laugh and make fun of me. I didn't think they would understand and would think I was being a baby because I was sad about my mom going away.

Maybe this counselor would help me figure out my feelings. I was so confused by everything that was going on inside of me.

When we got to the counselor's office, I was getting nervous because I didn't know her. In the parking lot, I was thinking about how the counselor would look, what her office would look like, and if she was nice. When we got inside, we rode an old elevator to the third floor and got off. I had never been on an elevator that old. My mom, dad, and I worried that we wouldn't make it to the top.

We met Miss Cynthia at the door to her office. She looked close to how I imagined. She had dark hair, wasn't very tall, and seemed friendly. We introduced ourselves and sat down. She had a fun office with several toys, artwork, and lots of books. My mom and dad sat on the couch. I asked Miss Cynthia if I could sit at her desk. She agreed. Once we all sat down, we started talking about our feelings.

Miss Cynthia asked me how I felt about the deployment and I said I was mad, sad, and frustrated. I was mad because I didn't want my mom to leave for six months, I was sad because I love my mom and I wouldn't be able to see her for a long time, and I was frustrated because she had to go into war with other people. I was also scared for my mom's safety.

Miss Cynthia asked me if I would do a journal about my feelings. She said that I had a good way of expressing myself and that journaling might help. I was a little scared about writing a journal at first because I didn't think I was that good at writing about my feelings, but I decided to take the opportunity to do it. Miss Cynthia also asked Mom to do the same thing and write a journal about her feelings while preparing for the deployment and while she was gone. Miss Cynthia thought that we could try to turn our journals into a book that could be shared with other kids who learn about their mom going on a deployment.

At the end of the session, I felt happy because I knew that my mom would help me, and I knew we could do this together. I was also happy because Miss Cynthia was nice. It was not too difficult to talk to her about my feelings. She made it feel all right.

After we left, I asked my mom if we could really do a book, and my mom told me that she would make it happen if that was what I really wanted. When she said that, I believed it would happen because my mom always does what she says she is going to do.

Chapter 2

FIDGET SPINNERS AND ARMY GUYS

Over the next several days, I didn't really think too much about the deployment because I focused on other stuff, like school and my friends. Then I would start to think about it at night before bed because that was the time when my mind wasn't focused on school or other things. I felt sadder at night when I thought about my family and the deployment. I wished I could keep my mind busy all the time so that I wouldn't focus on it, but that just wasn't possible.

The following week, I noticed that I was thinking about the deployment more during the day, and every time I would get it off my mind, something would remind me of it again. For example, on Thursday before we left for my piano lesson, my mom told me that I should work on my deployment journal. I immediately got sad in my mind. I tried to get it out of my head, but nothing worked. Then, the following Saturday morning, we did a charity run for the police department bike patrol. After the run, my mom again told me that I should write about it in my journal. I felt like crying because it reminded me about the deployment, which she would be leaving for in seven months.

In May, my mom told me that she had to go to combat readiness training. This training was supposed to be something that helped her get ready for her deployment, but it felt like it was extra time away from me, which made me sad and angry again. I just wanted my mom to stay home forever with me and Dad. Whenever she is gone, it feels different in our house. It is not the same without my mom.

When the time came for my mom to go to training, I watched her pack her things. I tried to help her as much as I could. The morning came when she was leaving, and I felt nervous and scared because she was going to be gone for eight days. I gave her three hugs that day and asked her to take one of my toy army guys with her to keep her safe. Dad and I also made a card while Mom was in the bathroom getting ready. We hid the card in her folder so she would find it later. I really didn't want her to go, but I understood that she had to. I ran out to the garage to watch her drive away. The feeling of not having my mom with me is depressing because she can't make me feel secure. I know that she loves me more than anything because she always tells me that, but it is just not the same as having her with me.

Dad and I talked on the drive to school that morning and we discussed how we were going to do stuff during the week without her. Dad told me that it would be OK and that he would do all the things that Mom normally did. I felt better because I knew that my dad understood how I felt. Dad cried too for a little bit that morning, and I knew that he was just as sad as I was.

The first weekend after Mom left, Dad and I went to a party for someone that my dad works with. I saw my friend Keegan and some other kids at the party. We were able to play casino games and run around the yard. The party was fun because it helped me forget about my mom being away.

When we got home, Dad and I also played on the big dirt hills across the street from our house. These dirt hills were there because they were planning to build some new homes during the summer. When we were climbing, I almost fell off a couple times! Although it scared me, it was fun because I got to spend a lot of time with my dad. I realized that my dad was trying very hard to get the combat readiness training off both of our minds.

My dad told me that this was practice so both of us could prepare for when Mom would be deployed. As we headed into the week, I helped Dad in the morning by getting ready quickly and doing my chores for the cat. I also helped at night by going to bed without a fight, and I took showers as quickly as possible. I even dried out the shower when I was done using it. I was helping Dad because I wanted to show him that the two of us could cooperate during the deployment.

When Mom called for the first time, I felt like jumping up and down for joy because I got to see her on video chat for the first time in three days. She hadn't called too much during the first three days because she was too busy with things.

Mom did a couple fun things for me while she was away. She took pictures of the army guy that I had given her and texted them to me. I had to try and find the army guy, who was hidden in several of the places where she was. He was hard to find in most of the pictures, but some of them were easy. I found them all except for one. I still haven't found it to this day. Mom also sent me a picture of a glow-in-the-dark fidget spinner. It was green and cool. When Mom called me that night, she told me that the fidget spinner was one of the instructors' and he said that I could have it. I was so happy because now I would have two fidget spinners, and one of them would be from a military guy that had done a lot of deployments and trainings. It was special to me because it was from the leader of military training.

On the day that Mom came home, I was excited and happy because I would see her in real life. It was Mother's Day weekend, so I made something special at school that week for her. It was a pop-up card with flowers inside. Dad and I also bought some cards from the store to give Mom, along with some flowers. On the way home, Dad stopped and got Mom a gift card from the nail salon. We wanted to make Mother's Day as special as we could. Mom called while Dad was in the nail salon. I didn't tell her what Dad was doing so it could be a surprise.

I was using the Jaguar vehicle app on Dad's phone to spy on where Mom was. I could see that she was just leaving her base. She would be home in less than half an hour. We talked for most of her drive home, so when she pulled in the driveway, Dad and I were waiting for her. We hugged her for a long time. Dad helped her get her bags in from the car and Mom gave me the fidget spinner and my army guy. Everything felt right in the house again.

At bedtime that night, it started to feel different because it wasn't just Dad and I anymore. Although I was happy to have Mom back, I now had two people telling me to get ready for bed and brush my teeth. It feels like it is two against one sometimes. Mom seemed different to me, too. She was tired and more easily frustrated with me. She told me that it was because she was physically and mentally tired and she needed a few days to recover. I tried to understand what that meant, but I really didn't. I just wanted Mom to be back to her regular self.

The next couple of days were a little rough because it kind of seemed like she was carrying on with how she had been at combat readiness training. She was rougher than she normally is around the house. This made me act different towards her, too. I started being meaner towards her. But after a few days and lots of talks, we got back to our happy family. I learned that life doesn't always go your way and there are twists and turns in it, but if you make the best of it with your family, you can straighten out the road.

Another great thing happened during the weekend when Mom got home. I found out that I won second place at the state level for the American Legion Essay Contest. My essay won first place in the school district and then it had been sent on to the state level. I received a letter and a certificate in the mail letting me know I was a second-place winner. I also received a check for $25.00. The thing that made me most proud was that the essay was about patriotism and everyone doing their part. My mom was going to live her part soon with the deployment. It also meant a lot because I received the letter on Mother's Day weekend, so I know I made my mom proud. I felt so good because I won for something that was written about my mom. It was funny because my mom had just gotten back from combat readiness training, too.

Chapter 3

SORRY WEEDS

A week or so after my mom returned from her readiness training, we had a second visit with Miss Cynthia. I felt more comfortable this time because I had talked with her before. I knew how she acted and her personality. I sat in the same desk chair and played with some of her toys. I brought up the combat readiness training and how it felt to be with just my dad and I (and my cat) for a week. She asked me questions about how it felt to be alone with just Dad, and I said it was fun because each night we would play football or do something together. We also talked about my thoughts on my mom being gone.

I told Miss Cynthia that I still felt sad. I talked about how different it felt when Mom came home from her training because it seemed like she was a stranger. Mom and Dad didn't understand this at first, but Miss Cynthia did a good job of explaining my feelings to them. She said that maybe Mom is not the same person when she comes home because she is stressed and tired. She said I can sense when my mom feels this way, and it makes me kind of feel the same way. I told

Miss Cynthia that I was doing my journal and that I was on the fourth or fifth page. Mom, Dad, and I left the visit feeling good because I got all my emotions out. It was a good session.

After that, Mom had a Guard weekend like she normally does, and for the most part, it went well. Dad always talks to me about how to make our lives easier and not cause problems because Mom is usually tired when she gets home. I try my best to do my part, but sometimes I fail at that because I want things my way and I want to play on the iPad. Also, I just sometimes forget.

After the Guard weekend, it was the last week of school. I felt good because I knew that summer vacation was here. On the last day of school, it was awesome because we only had a half-day. All we had to do was play word search and look at our essays. We also had to answer some questions about our teacher. Mom and Dad both came to pick me up. It was a little weird because usually I don't have both parents at pick up. Mom had a sign that she made for me, and she was jumping for joy because I made it through the third grade. I was happy and embarrassed at the same time. I also felt very sad because I wouldn't get to see half of my friends over the summer. Mom seemed kind of sad because she knew she would not be there the following year for my graduation from fourth grade.

I was not being the nicest kid that afternoon, so Dad talked to me about giving Mom opportunities to be with me as much as possible until her deployment. We went out to eat for lunch and then we went to an escape room, which was so much fun. Mom and Dad also gave me some gifts, which I liked.

I was in a grumpy mood for the next couple of days, but I couldn't figure out why. Maybe it was because I was thinking about when Mom wouldn't be there to see me graduate from the fourth grade. When I let my mind wander, it seemed like I thought about sad things.

On Saturday morning, the weekend after school ended, I was watching videos on my iPad. I came across an ad that said, "After you watch these videos, you will hate Justin Bieber." I decided to watch it anyway because I didn't really like Justin Bieber to begin with. I clicked on the video and I saw him being mean to a bunch of people. There was one video where he pushed a cameraman and one where he yelled at people, but the one that really upset me was the one with a special needs person. In this video, Justin ignored the person that was special needs and took pictures with everyone else. I started to cry because it was so unfair and mean to someone who has special needs.

I was crying on the couch and Mom came home and saw me. She asked what was wrong and I told her about the video. Mom told me that I should not watch those things and that some people just don't know how to act around special needs people. I continued to be pretty upset and sat in my room by myself for a while. I couldn't get past it for some reason because it was just so mean. Mom told me that I should be proud of myself because I was a kind-hearted boy. She told me that there are not a lot of boys who care this much, and this was one of the reasons she was so proud of me.

We talked about it a little while longer, and then she made me come outside to help her pull weeds. Even though I was still sad, I went outside with Mom and took my sadness out on the weeds. After a little while, I was laughing again because pulling weeds was helping me deal with my anger and sadness at Justin Bieber. I was happy Mom was there to talk to me. She knows how to help me talk things out. I would miss that when she was gone.

Chapter 4

WAR GAMES

Even before she found out about the deployment, my mom had been doing classes for the military. It made me frustrated because, for eighteen months, she had always been working on school work at night and on the weekends. I was proud that my mom was giving her all to something, but I was also sad because she couldn't just play with Dad and me. Then, a couple weeks after I was done with school, my mom finished her classes. She was so happy! We went out to eat at Su Casa, a Mexican restaurant near our house. She had a margarita and was acting funny after drinking it. I had never seen her like that before. I didn't really like my mom being this goofy. I guess the alcohol had something to do with it, huh?

I was happy that my mom finished her classes because it meant we could spend more time together before she left on her deployment. Watching my mom go through her classes taught me that you have to try hard at everything you do, even if you don't like it. I had even helped my mom with one of the tests. It was difficult, but it was interesting because it was like a war video game.

She would sit for hours in the kitchen and get really frustrated with some of the classes. She almost cried once or twice because she was struggling to pass some of the tests. It was hard to watch her struggle. I felt bad for her. I would think about it at night when I was going to sleep. I wanted to help her as much as I could because it didn't seem fair. She worked so hard at stuff.

From watching my mom, I learned that I need to go "all in" on my schoolwork, too. If she can do it, so can I. I decided I would work hard while she was gone to show her that she can be proud of me, too.

A couple years previously, Mom had asked me to come up with a personal brand. I didn't know what she was talking about, but she explained it to me. She said it was a description of what I wanted people to think about me. I knew right away what I wanted it to be. I said, "All in." She was surprised by my response. Both she and Dad smiled. They liked it. I said, "I want people to know that I go all in on everything I'm doing." I think my dad is still thinking about what his personal brand is.

The first weekend in July, my mom and I were hanging out together and having fun. She was joking around with me, but at some point, I didn't like it anymore. She was trying to have fun, but I thought she was trying to pick on me. After a few minutes, I got annoyed and I said something that I would come to regret. I said, "I wish you were already in Qatar." I was trying to joke around, but I got too serious and said something that I absolutely did not mean. I was frustrated that Mom was picking on me. Well, I THOUGHT she was picking on me, and I didn't know how to take it. I know that she was trying to have fun, but I was getting hurt by it.

We talked about it right away. I felt horrible about what I had said because I never would have meant it seriously. I did not want my mom to go, and sometimes I just didn't know how to handle it. My frustration sometimes came out in ways that I didn't think were good, but I wasn't sure how to control it.

Mom and I both cried, and I said "sorry" at least five times. I kept looking at Mom to make sure she was OK. I never wanted to hurt my mom. I know I did, and that was one of the worst things I could have done. When Mom and Dad joke with me in the future, I am going to try and have more fun with it. I have thought about it a few times since it happened, and I still feel bad. I guess I am still learning.

The second weekend of July, I had my best friend, Sam, sleep over. When he was here, my mom and dad put three clocks in my room that were set to the time in Menomonee Falls, Wisconsin; Washington, D.C.; and Al Udeid, Qatar. When I saw them, I asked my mom why there were three clocks in my room. She said she wanted me to be able to see all the different times for where she would be when she was gone. When I asked about Washington, D.C., she and Dad said it is the capital of the Armed Services. The clocks were VERY cool, and it was neat to see what time it was in Qatar compared to Wisconsin. I thought the ticking was going to be annoying, but when I went to bed the following night with Mom lying next to me, it was calming. It sounded kind of like the cocking of a gun because the second hands ticked loudly and went one right after the other.

It was neat to have my room set up like a command center of the military. I told Mom that all we needed was a circular table for all the military leaders to sit around. I know about the command centers from movies and my mom. She tells me about how she works in the command center when they do exercises at her base. As a Commander, she gets to be part of a lot of these things.

Chapter 5

ICE BEAR

In August, I signed up for a new flag football league. My team's name was the NY Giants. I started practicing on a Thursday, and my first game was Friday. It didn't give us much time to learn plays but that was OK. I enjoy football, and I thought playing would help me keep all the deployment stuff off my mind. I hoped I would have a good season and like the other boys on the team. Because this was a new league, I knew I would most likely not know too many kids, so that had me nervous.

When football started, my cat, Ice Bear, had been sick for about a week. We took him to the vet over the weekend to try and figure out what was wrong with him. He had to have an IV put in, so the vet shaved one of his legs to insert the needle. It made me want to cry when I first saw him. He wouldn't eat, so we had to take him back to the vet again two days later. I felt scared about his health. It also made me scared to think about losing him and not having him in our family, especially with Mom going overseas. If we were to lose Ice Bear, it would only be Dad and me during the deployment.

I like having Bear in my family because he is funny and makes me feel good inside when I pet him and snuggle with him. He is fun to play with, and he likes to go outside and hunt birds and frogs. I told Mom and Dad that the happiest day of my life was when I got Ice Bear. I feel like his big brother because I get to take care of him.

It seemed like I thought more about my mom leaving whenever I would get sad about other things, like Bear. Maybe it was because when I was sad about one thing, I also thought about other sad things. I wished I didn't have to think about any of that!

We said prayers asking if God could help Ice Bear get better. I kept my fingers crossed about Bear's health and waited to hear back from the vet. A day later, a call came in and we learned that Bear had to have surgery. He was getting blocked when he was trying to go to the bathroom. The vet said the surgery was standard for male Bombay cats, which is what Bear is. I didn't think I would sleep until we had Bear back with us.

The following week was a good week because Bear came home, got his stitches out, and got his cone taken off his head. He started to get back to normal, which made me happy. I was so glad that he was getting better. He is an important part of my family, and if he is in pain, I feel the pain, too.

That week was also good because Mom and Dad took a half-day off work so we could go to the State Fair. It was fun to spend the day together, but I also thought about what the next year would be like. This would be the time of year when my mom would just be coming home from her deployment. It seemed like a long time before she would get home.

We did all the normal things at the State Fair; we played games, won stuffed animals, ate a lot of food, and rode a few rides. I loved the game where I shot the gun and tried to take out the red star that was on a piece of paper down at the other end. They used a pulley string to bring the target to me when I was finished, which was fun to watch. I won the biggest teddy bear. It was almost as tall as me.

The last reason this week was so good was that I got to go to my mom's Air Force base, the 128th Air Refueling Wing. We went because my dad needed to renew his military ID. Driving on the base was cool because I saw barricades and barbwire fences. I asked Dad what they were for, and he explained that it was to protect the base if anyone tried to drive onto it that was not supposed to.

I got to see the planes while we were there. My mom said they were C-135s. One was in the hanger getting worked on by maintenance guys. Going into my mom's office was cool because I got to see what she does when she is gone for the weekend.

It was neat to see other guys in uniforms, like my mom. It made me think that I might want to go into the military one day when I get older, too. I think being in the military would be awesome because you get to use guns. Your job is to protect our country.

My mom couldn't stay with us for very long because she had a meeting to go to with a colonel. When Dad and I left the base, we had to exit out the secret back side of the base because they were doing construction at the main gate. My mom said they were installing a camera and making the base safer for all the airmen. We got to drive under two runways on the way out, too. It was crazy to think about planes taking off over our heads. My mom told me that the following year, when I turned ten years old, I would be able to get my own ID card. I was excited to have my own.

A week or so after my dad got his ID card, my mom was out doing more training for her deployment. She had to spend the entire week out at her base. She got to shoot guns, practice putting on her chemical gear and gas mask, and learn about the culture in Qatar, the country that she was deploying to. My mom brought home a couple bullet shells for me to keep. One was from an M4 and the other was from a 9mm pistol. She had to qualify on both guns. She had to shoot two to the chest and one to the head for kill shots on all targets. My mom also showed me a video of her shooting the M4 on rapid fire. I was proud because not everyone's mom gets to do this stuff. It is unreal to think about my mom protecting our country. I know my mom is going to be safe because, like she said, she is too smart to get hurt.

Chapter 6

NERVES AND VOMIT

It happened. I had to register for the fourth grade at Riverside Elementary. It was hard to believe the summer would be coming to an end soon. It didn't seem fair. My mom was able to leave early from her military training so she could come with Dad and me to register. I got to meet my teacher and see everyone in my class. It made me think about my mom leaving because school starting just meant it was that much closer to her deployment.

The following week during my piano lesson, I was hoping to play one of the songs good for my mom. She had listened to me practice the weekend before and started crying because she said that I played it so well. She started thinking about leaving and got pretty broken up. She cried and said she didn't want to go on the deployment. This was hard for me to watch. I never know what to do to make it better when she cries. So, at my piano lesson, I was trying hard to play that song good for her again.

I asked her to listen from the other room, and when I started to play, I made some mistakes. I immediately started crying because I wanted to make my mom proud of me. I was crying hard, so my mom ended up coming in by me to see if I was OK. I told her that I loved her so much and I didn't want her to leave. My mom hugged me for a little bit until I stopped crying. She took me into the bathroom and helped me calm down. My teacher asked me to try it one more time, and I did it! I wasn't sure where all the emotions came from, but I had to let it out.

When my mom and I left, we started crying again, and we talked in the car for a little bit. My mom made me feel better by telling me that she was going to be OK. My mom had asked me to play a song about America on the piano when she got back from Qatar, so I thought it was important to do good at piano before she left. Making my mom proud is important to me.

I asked her not to tell Dad about the crying because I didn't want him to get sad. My dad gets upset a lot about Mom leaving, so I didn't want him to know that I wasn't being strong. My mom told me that I didn't need to be strong, I just needed to be me, and if I felt sad at times, that was OK. We made sure to clear our tears before we pulled into the driveway that night. Dad was waiting for us outside and playing basketball. I don't think Mom ever told Dad about it. I tried to put it out of my head after we got home.

Another Guard weekend came for my mom and she had to miss my flag football game. She made a sign to cheer me on since she wasn't going to be there. On the sign, she wrote a note that said I would get $5.00 if I got a flag. I thought it was nice of her to do that, but at the same time, it made me more nervous because I didn't want to let her down. Dad added more to the dollar amount, so it made me even more nervous. I sometimes feel these nerves inside of me and they are hard to control. It almost makes me feel sick. I think it is because I worry about not doing a good job.

When we pulled up at the field, I had a lot of butterflies in my stomach. I wished Mom was there so she could help me calm down. Dad kept telling me that it was going to be OK, but I was still feeling sick with nerves and the fear of getting hurt.

When the game started, I got really tensed up and couldn't get into the game. I felt like I didn't want to be out there. When I looked back at Dad, I started to feel a little better because I knew he would always be there for me. Unfortunately, my nerves got the best of me and I threw up on the field. It got all over my chin strap, cleats, gloves, shirt, and the ground. At that moment, I felt like Dad would be very, very disappointed in me.

One of the referees came on to the field and asked if I was OK. I told him, "No." He walked me off to the sideline and Coach Mark came to check on me. I sat on the bench and took my helmet off. Dad came by me. He looked mad at first but asked if I was OK. He told me that we needed to do things his way for games, not my way, because he thought I threw up because of what I ate before the game. I told him that it was nerves. I sat out for about ten plays and then I got back in the game.

I was able to finish the game and did a pretty good job on defense. I think Dad ended up happy with me because I was trying my best. After the game, Nana came over by us and yelled at my dad because she felt like he was being too hard on me. Dad got upset and we eventually went home. When we got there, he made me write about my nerves and what we needed to do differently. After everything was done, I felt like I had let him down bad. Dad told me that we needed to talk to Mom about it when she got home.

A few hours later, I heard Mom upstairs. It was a little while before she came down by me and asked about the game. I sat on her lap and told her about everything. It felt different talking to Mom about it than it did with Dad. It seemed like Mom didn't get as mad, but she got sad.

I learned that I have to fight through things sometimes to make myself and others proud. I felt like some of the nerves came from knowing my mom was deploying. All my emotions were crazy. If my mom hadn't been going away, I don't think I would have been so nervous and scared out on the field.

The next week, I continued to not feel the best. It wasn't my nerves anymore. I got sick on Tuesday of that week. Mom was traveling again for work, so Dad stayed home with me. It must have been the flu bug. Mom came home on Wednesday and she stayed with me that day. Mom asked me questions about football and how I was feeling about it. I told her that I was still nervous about the upcoming game. I was scared about getting hurt and letting my coach and teammates down.

Mom told me that we were going to see Miss Cynthia again on Friday night, and that made me happy. I liked talking to her about my emotions. Miss Cynthia was good at understanding me when I explained things to her. Mom thought it was a good idea to talk to Miss Cynthia about how my nerves had been.

Friday night came, and we all met at Miss Cynthia's office. We sat down and I started to talk about the game when I had thrown up on the field. Miss Cynthia asked how I felt about it, and I told her that I felt better after throwing up because it felt like some of the nerves got out of me. She told me that I should do some deep breaths before the game the next day and tell myself, "Just relax." She said I should repeat it over and over again until I felt better. I agreed to try it. We also talked more about Mom's deployment getting closer and closer and that maybe that was part of the problem, too. I told her that all my emotions were crazy.

After Miss Cynthia's, I felt a little bit better going into the night. But when I woke up in the morning, I felt sick again.

It just kept getting worse as the minutes ticked by. Mom and Dad started to get upset because they thought we were on the right track after talking to Miss Cynthia. They decided that we would call the coach and let him know that I was sick. Dad also called Nana for the first time after their fight and told her that I was sick and not playing in the game that day. We all felt bad for the rest of the day because we knew that this issue was really, really frustrating. Mom and Dad had been trying everything to help me get over my fears, but nothing was working. I felt bad inside because I was letting my mom and dad down. I loved playing football more than anything, and I didn't want my career to be over, but I couldn't control my fears inside. We tried to get our minds off it, but it seemed impossible that weekend.

Chapter 7

A BIG DECISION

The next week, things were kind of back to normal at first, but on Tuesday, when Mom was driving me to the before and after school program, Kids Inc., she asked me if I wanted to stop playing football. I felt like I wanted to say "yes," but another part of me wanted to say "no." We continued to talk for a little bit in the parking lot. I told her that I didn't want my friends to be mad at me, and she told me that my friends would understand, especially my best friend Sam. She said that he was my best friend and he has always been a good friend, like when I struggled with riding my bike, he told me that he fell off a lot when he was learning, too. Mom said this would be no different. Since Sam was playing on the same team this fall, he would miss playing with me, but we would still be friends.

Mom asked me the question one more time about quitting football, and I said, "I want to quit."

Mom said, "OK. Think about it today and we can talk to Dad tonight."

I asked Mom if she could tell Dad before he picked me up that night, and she agreed. I felt pretty good after making the decision, and I think Mom did too. So during recess, I decided to tell one of my friends on the team, Matthew, and he said he was fine with it. He didn't even seem to care. That made me feel even better because he wasn't mad at all. I still had to tell Sam, but that could wait for another day.

When Dad picked me up from Kids Inc., he asked me how my day was. I told him it was good. He then asked me if I was quitting football, and I told him yes. He seemed OK with it and stated that he was fine as long as I was happy. That night, it finally felt good at home. I felt like I had a huge problem off my shoulders. We agreed to think about it until Saturday morning. If it still felt like the right decision at that time, we would call Coach Mark and let him know.

During lunch at school on Thursday, Matthew yelled to Sam that I was going to quit football. Sam asked me at recess if it was true, and I told him yes. Sam asked me if I was thinking about playing tackle football with the Junior Indians team the next year and I said no. The Junior Indians is a local team that some kids join when they want to do tackle football instead of flag. He also asked me why I was quitting, and I told him that I was struggling from a health standpoint. My nerves were really getting bad. He seemed to understand. I was relieved because my best friend was not mad at me, just like Mom had said. I had thought in my head that EVERYONE would be mad at me, but in the end, no one was. I was starting to feel like this decision was the best one I had ever made for myself.

Saturday came and I stayed firm with my decision. Dad made the call to Coach Mark and explained that I was quitting the team. Coach Mark asked if it had anything to do with anyone on the team or with him as a coach. Dad explained that it didn't have anything to do with that. It was something personal and that I had a lot of stuff going on to deal with. Coach Mark said he understood. He also said that I was a good player and he would love to coach me again in the future if I changed my mind. That made me feel good to hear.

Dad then called Nana and told her as well. They still hadn't really talked about the fight, but she seemed happy to hear that football was over. I don't think she understood everything that was going on with my feelings about football, nerves, fears, and the deployment. Dad and Mom talked about how to deal with Nana, and they agreed to give it some time.

The rest of the weekend felt awesome! It really seemed like Mom and Dad were happy about my decision. That made me feel so relieved. I hate disappointing my parents because I love them so much!

Chapter 8

ABE LINCOLN
AND BRACES

In the next couple of weeks, we talked about some other sports I could do, and I choose to get a personal trainer and a swimming instructor. I felt better about those sports because I couldn't get hurt as badly as I could playing football. That was my big fear with football.

Two weeks after I decided to quit football, we had an appointment with Miss Cynthia. I was happy to see her again. It was becoming comfortable going to her office. I wanted to talk to her about football and about my decision to do some other sports. When we got to her office, we all went inside and sat down. I started talking about football. I told her that I quit the team because of the stress I was feeling with the games. We also talked about the deployment. Miss Cynthia said that maybe the deployment was playing into my nerves, which is exactly what I had thought, too. She said that the decision was probably good. If my nerves were getting so bad that they made me sick, it was my body's way of telling me something wasn't right.

It was a short session for Dad and me. We left, and Mom stayed behind to talk to Miss Cynthia on her own. I didn't want to leave because I wanted to stay with Mom and play with Miss Cynthia's toys, but Dad told me that we should let Mom have her time. When Mom got home, she said that it felt good to talk to somebody about it. I was happy to hear that she could talk about the deployment with someone and still feel happy at the same time.

I started my personal training with Luke the following week at the gym my dad goes to. The first session was focused on my balance and footwork. These workouts made me feel better about myself because I got stronger and more athletic. They also felt good because I liked working with one person, not groups. I liked the one-on-one interaction way better. I still had not started swimming, but I was looking forward to that, too.

When I came home from my workout, Mom told me that she had received an email from the person she was going to replace overseas. His name was Abraham (Abe for short), which my mom thought was funny because her father (my grandpa), who passed away before I was born, had been nicknamed Abe. This was because he looked like Abraham Lincoln. He had a dark beard and dark hair. I had seen pictures of him from my mom, and my grandpa did look like Lincoln. My mom thought it was a sign from Grandpa letting her know that she was going to be OK while she was deployed. I felt so good, too, knowing that Grandpa would be watching out for her.

When I came home from school one night the following week, Mom and Dad told me they had met with the orthodontist earlier that day. They told me I had to get braces. I was worried because I knew braces would hurt. Mom and Dad told me it was better to get braces now instead of when I am older because it would be easier and faster. They told me that I was going to get braces on my lower teeth and a spacer on my top teeth. I also had to wear headgear each night. My dad said that he was going to have to turn a screw in my mouth every night to widen my teeth and jaw. I thought this sounded crazy.

My mom felt bad because she was going to be gone for most of the process. I would have my braces for twelve months total, and my mom would be gone for seven of those months! She could tell I was scared, so she shared with me how she felt when she got braces and explained more about it. It made me feel better because someone else that I knew had gone through it. My mom said she was even more excited to get back from her deployment now so she could see my straight teeth.

Things had been going well all week until Thursday, when I had my piano lesson. We had to go to a parent-teacher conference first, but my teacher was running late and Dad and I couldn't stay. Mom stayed behind to talk to my teacher so Dad could take me to piano. Dad didn't stay for most of the piano lesson because he had to run errands. During the lesson with Miss Garcia, I was having fun for the most part. When Dad got back, I started to get a little off track. I was playing a patriotic song because I wanted to learn one for my mom's deployment.

I was singing the song when Dad came back, and he got upset at me because he thought I was not being respectful to Miss Garcia. He thought I was not listening and not doing my best. He asked me on a scale of one to ten how my lesson was for focus, and I said it was a seven. Miss Garcia gave me a score of six or seven. So, on the drive home, Dad talked to me. He said I was not giving my all to the lessons. He told me that I had to go home and practice piano for fifteen extra minutes. I felt sad about it because I thought I did fine at piano. It confused me.

When we walked in the door, I changed into my pajamas and started playing piano. Mom came down to listen to me and I started to cry because I didn't want her to get mad at me, too. I had started thinking about her deployment again. Why did that always happen? Whenever I was upset about something, I thought about her leaving. She hugged me and let me cry for a while. It felt good to have her hugs.

Dad came down and I apologized to him. He said that he understood, but I needed to do the right thing. He and I hugged it out, and I felt better because Dad was not mad at me anymore. I just want the deployment to be over.

A couple weeks later, I got my braces on. It was on a Monday and Dad took me to the appointment. It took a long time because they had to get all the wet stuff (saliva) out of my mouth so the braces wouldn't slip off my teeth. The orthodontist made the braces on a mouth mold first and then stuck the braces onto my teeth. I was a little scared or nervous because I thought it was going to really hurt. After the appointment was done, I went back to school for the day. I told my friends about it and they thought it was pretty cool that I had braces.

My teeth started to hurt later that night. Mom and Dad gave me an ibuprofen to help with the pain. Mom gave me a big hug, and I started to cry because I wanted her to stay and help me through it. I felt like she was the only one who really felt my pain because she had gone through it, too. Mom told me that it was going to hurt for the first few days, but after that, it would get better. She also told me to eat softer foods and to chew on the side of my mouth instead. I felt better because Mom wouldn't lie to me. I trusted her. Just like Mom said, it started to feel a lot better a couple days later. I was not so sad then because the pain was gone. I just needed to figure out how to not get food caught in my braces.

I was still a bit sad that Mom wouldn't be there to help me through my braces, but I knew that I could be tough like her. If she could get deployed for seven months, I could figure out how to take control of my braces. I thought, "I got this for her!"

Chapter 9

BURNING THREADS

In my next training session with Luke, my dad came with me and learned the exercises, too. I liked it when Dad did the exercises because he had to learn new moves. We learned how to do towel pull-ups, leapfrog on the steps, and dips. My dad was really, really proud of me. We talked about continuing to do these workouts with Luke while Mom is away. Our goal was that by the time Mom returned, I would have some BIG muscles.

A couple days later, my piano lesson went very well. Mom was with me that time, and she was super proud. If Mom says I do good, then I believe it!

The following Saturday, my friend Ethan came over for a play date. We played Madden 18, which was something I earned for good behavior during the week. I owned my responsibilities, which is exactly what I would need to continue doing while Mom was gone. That would be the best way for me to help.

On Saturday night, I went to a birthday party at Garcade. It is an arcade place in our town. We had a sleepover at

Brandan's house. Some of my friends were wrestling during the night, and I got kicked in the nose. It hurt bad and blood started gushing out immediately. Brandan's mom and dad came upstairs to see what had happened. His dad got some napkins and sat me down in a chair, and his mom started cleaning up the floor. She told me to go into the bathroom to change my clothes. After I came out, she gave me an ice pack. I wanted to call my mom more than anything, but Brendan's mom told me that it was late and we should probably not call now. I was scared, but I thought about it and I calmed down. I decided to be strong and go watch a movie with my friends.

That same weekend, Mom got new uniforms for her deployment. They looked way different than her normal uniforms, which my mom called "ABUs." Her new ones had more of a jungle-looking camouflage and a bunch of Velcro patches for her name, rank, and the US flag. I thought the new uniforms looked way cooler than her other uniforms.

She asked me if I would help her burn off some of the threads that hang from new uniforms. She usually uses a lighter to burn the threads instead of cutting them off. I thought it would be fun to burn them off, so I helped. There were lots of them. She didn't really seem very happy to have to get a new set of uniforms ready for deployment. She had gotten her other ones all set, so this was just more work for her. The lighter ran out after a couple uniforms, so we had to finish them the next week.

Chapter 10

A STAR ON THE NEWS

My mom's birthday is usually around Thanksgiving. Dad and I wanted to do something special for it because she would be going away soon. So, for her birthday we got a flower vase, a big Styrofoam ball, and five pounds of Tootsie Pops. We made a bouquet and stuck all the Tootsie Pops into the Styrofoam ball on top of the vase. We tied an orange ribbon around the vase because she likes the color orange. We also put a balloon on top. Her favorite treat is a Tootsie Pop every night before bed, so we knew she would love this. When we gave it to her, my mom could not have been happier. She called it the best present ever.

There was also a flower that came with the vase. Dad and I planned to plant the flower and grow it while Mom was deployed. When she came home, it would be a beautiful, full-grown flower just for her.

We usually put up Christmas decorations right after Thanksgiving, but that year, Mom and Dad were debating about even putting up the decorations because she was leaving right after Christmas. I really wanted to put up the decorations, so I begged them to still do it. Eventually, Mom agreed because she wanted to make me happy. I agreed to help as much as possible. We started with the downstairs tree and we all worked together as a family, which is always a good feeling.

Over the next few days, we put up the upstairs tree and put decorations above the kitchen cabinets. It looked amazing when we were done. My favorite decoration was the tree upstairs because it was over ten feet tall and the ornaments were rustic and sparkly. I love the house at Christmas because it feels so warm and cozy. It makes me feel good to sit in our house around the holidays and look at the lights. We always play Christmas music and light candles, which also make the house feel warm. I did end up helping for some of it, but really, Mom did most of the work.

I was thankful for my mom because I knew she did it for me. She would do anything to make me happy, and that meant a lot to me. I thought, "Hopefully she is still here to help Dad and me clean it up after Christmas. Otherwise, it might be up till July when she comes home (ha-ha)."

The first weekend in December, Mom had Guard again. Man, that seemed like it came so quickly. There was a send-off ceremony at the base for all the deployers. There were over 150 deployers in total being sent from the 128th Air Refueling Wing. It made me feel proud that my mom was one of them, but I felt different inside sometimes because I was the only one in my school who had their mom going away.

The morning of the send-off ceremony, Dad left to get Mom some flowers. While he was gone, my relatives came to the house. They were coming with Dad and me to the base. It was my grandma, three aunts, and my uncle. They stayed for a little bit and looked at our house and decorations. They said everything was beautiful.

We left for the ceremony and Aunt Lori followed my dad to the base. When we got there, we had to park off base and take a shuttle. I thought the bus looked like a prison bus. It reminded me of the bus from the *Fast and Furious* movies, which are my favorite movies. Dad was trying to be funny and said that maybe Dom, one of the main characters from the movie, was on the bus. Dad sometimes thinks he is funny, but he really isn't (ha-ha). We had to wait fifteen minutes just to get on the bus. Once we got on the base, the bus dropped us off at one of the hangars. The hangar is the building where they work on the airplanes. The ceremony was going to be inside the hangar.

When I walked in, the first thing I saw was a large United States flag. It was the biggest one I have ever seen. There was a band, and lots of people and soldiers were lined up. They seated us in one of the back rows, and it took me a while to actually find Mom. She was in formation with a bunch of other soldiers. It looked really cool to see all the soldiers lined up in seven rows. I noticed that some of the soldiers had different uniforms than my mom. I thought that it was odd, but I quickly realized that where they were getting deployed determined what color of camouflage they wore.

When the music and ceremony started, a general came up on stage and talked about the bravery that the soldiers had. He talked about how proud we should be and how it takes a family to get through a deployment. I felt REALLY proud that I have a mom who is so brave. Dad started tearing up several times. My mom's family was so proud of her, too. Most of them had never even been on an Air Force base. I had been on the base at least eight times.

The governor, Governor Walker, was also present. He was on the stage and talked about Wisconsin and how thankful he was to the soldiers for serving our country. After the ceremony, a representative from the military base asked my mom if the three of us would be on the news. My mom agreed, but I didn't really want to do it. They hooked a microphone onto Mom and asked her most of the questions. I thought she did really good. She never seems nervous to talk to people even if she doesn't know them. They told us that it would air on the news later that evening.

We were able to take pictures with Governor Walker. It was neat to meet him. I have the picture on my phone to prove to my friends that it happened. We don't always believe each other so this was my proof. We also got to take pictures as a family out by one of the planes, which was awesome. I got a few things given to me from the Red Cross and other organizations. One gift was a stuffed GI dog named Josh and the other was a bendable star man. I thought they treated the soldiers' kids well.

That night, I had my best friend Sam come over for a sleepover. It was nice to be able to hang out with my best friend. He had a brace on his leg then, so it was like both of us were going through some hard times. We were always there for each other.

We were watching the news occasionally to see if my family made it on TV. I was nervous to see if I was being watched by the whole world. The station that interviewed us was TMJ4 in Milwaukee. There was a small piece about the send-off ceremony at 6:00 p.m., but we were not on. At 10:00 p.m., while Mom was already sleeping, Dad called me upstairs because we were on TV. Dad recorded it for Mom to see in the morning.

I was shocked to see myself on the news. They asked me what my name was, and I spelled it for them. They showed the part where Mom talked about our journaling. They also showed the part where Mom said she worries more about Dad and me then she does about herself. This just showed how much she cares about us.

It was hard to believe sometimes that all this stuff was happening to me. My mom was deploying to defend our country and we were on TV because of it. My mom had given me experiences that so many children will NEVER have. I was really proud of that part of my life. I knew I would never forget it!

That Sunday night, when Mom got home from Guard, I was feeling mad. I think it was because it was a Sunday night and I knew I had to go to school the next day, but it was also because my mom is gone so much because of her Guard weekends. When we were downstairs in the TV room, my mom asked to see the car that I had colored with Sam the night before. I picked up the paper and threw it at her. Dad got pretty upset at me and told me that I wasn't doing my part as a family member. He told me to get it together and do the right thing.

I thought about why I had done that to my mom and I realized that I had taken my anger out on her. I didn't know why I did that sometimes. I had these feelings inside that made me mad. I just wanted my mom and dad to be with me.

Chapter 11

THE CRATE

The next week, my mom's crate came for her to ship her things over to Qatar. The crate was about the size of me. It was gray in color and it had four holes for the locks. The locks were orange. The lock passcode was 1224, and all of them had the same code. We chose that code because it was my mom's passcode on her phone and something easy for her to remember. I tested all the locks to make sure that they worked.

It felt cool to have my mom's things locked so no one else could get in, but I felt bad because she had to have half of her things taken away from her even though she was still here. I could tell that it was hard for Mom to plan this all out. She seemed fine on the outside, but I knew inside she was feeling sad. I can just tell with my mom when she is sad. It is how she talks and the look in her eye.

It seemed like my mom was packing everything. She had her uniforms, her hair dryer, and a ton of other things. My dad was going to ship it overseas on the following Monday. It had to be less than seventy pounds in order to meet the shipping requirements.

The next Monday came and my dad said we just made it with sixty-five pounds. My mom seemed happy once the big crate was shipped, until the next week when she realized she had sent something she shouldn't have. One morning, she figured out that she had mailed all the Velcro tags with her name, rank, and branch of service. She said she thought she had left one out for when she flew over, but she hadn't. She seemed so frustrated with herself for making a big mistake like this. She called Sergeant Mussa at her base and she helped my mom by ordering new ones that would hopefully get here in time for my mom to leave, which was in three weeks. If not, I guessed my mom would have to fly over wearing a different uniform. My fingers were crossed that they got here in time. If not, my mom could be in big trouble.

During this same week, one of my brackets for my braces came loose. I asked my mom and dad to look at it, and they thought we should call Dr. Daub to check on what we should do. My mom was going in to get a new retainer because she broke hers. She said she would talk to Dr. Daub about my bracket while she was there. After Mom went to her appointment, she said I had to go in as soon as possible.

Dad made an appointment for Thursday. When I got there, I was scared because I thought it was going to hurt my teeth again. I was right. The only good thing about it was that I got to change the color of my rubber bands. I had originally chosen a color to look like a gold rush, but it just looked like plain old yellow, so I changed the color to blue. I liked the look of the blue better. I decided it could be fun to change the colors sometimes. Dr. Daub also told me that my teeth were moving along quickly so I might have the braces removed before my mom came home. That was crazy to think about because it seemed fast for my braces to be over but a long time for my mom to be gone. The way I felt about time was confusing. It seemed like time went fast when I liked something and was having fun but slow when I was not. Why was that?

Chapter 12

THE SURPRISE

One night during the week after I got my braces fixed, my mom called Dad and me on the way home from work like she always does, and she said she had some special news. She asked me to get my pajamas on and eat fast so we could talk about it. I was feeling really excited inside because I thought my mom was going to tell me that she didn't have to go away. By the time she got home, I had done everything that I needed to. She sat down next to me and she said that the journal I was working on could get turned into a book. I thought that was cool, but I was so upset because I thought it was going to be that she didn't have to go on her deployment.

My face must have shown my disappointment because she asked me what was wrong. When I told her, she felt really bad that I'd thought that. She said she was sorry.

My mom said that there was a guy who was going to talk to someone in Chicago about the book. I wondered who was going to publish it. I asked when it was going to happen and if I would have to go to Chicago while she was gone. My mom told me that maybe Dad and I could take the train there if we needed to go while she was gone. We had done that before and it was fun. It takes about an hour and a half to get there. My mom said that nothing was for sure, but the guy that she talked to was so nice for even thinking of helping us with our book. She said we should be thankful.

Dad said it was cool that I was doing this for other kids or families that will have to go through deployment in the future. He said he was super proud of me. I felt proud of myself, too, because it would be special to have a nine-year-old boy publish a book. My mom said that we could work with some people who could help me do pictures in the book. That sounded fun. Mom and Dad both seemed so happy and excited. My mom said that the guy was going to talk to the company on Tuesday, so we find out more stuff after that.

This same week, my report card came home. I was nervous to share it with Mom and Dad because I didn't want to have any bad grades. Mom and Dad let me open it, and I read it to them while we sat in the kitchen. I had straight A's and my teacher said it was a pleasure to have me in her class. I felt pumped after that. Mom and Dad were more than excited and proud of me. It made feel good that I was able to accomplish this for my mom and dad, especially before my mom left. This showed that I was truly "all in" on school. I was doing my part to help. My mom didn't have to worry about me! As I had said before, "I got this!"

The next exciting thing was that my class was planning a party for my mom before she left on deployment. Leading up to the party, my class made flags out of popsicle sticks, colored our desks red, white and blue, and made a video for her. The video was of all my classmates sending a message to my mom. They talked about how thankful they were for her to serve our country and how proud they were. They also said that they were going to take care of me while my mom was gone.

My teacher, Mrs. Halleen, put the messages to music, and my dad had sent her a picture of Mom and me to put in the video.

The day finally came for the party. I was excited because my mom was coming. I like having parties, and this one was about my mom and me. When my mom got there, everyone clapped for her. She was able to wear her deployment uniform because her name tags arrived quickly. I was happy about that for her. She sat next to me as we showed her the video. She started crying and said that it was so special. Some of my friends' parents came to the party as well to show their support. My mom thought that was really nice. My mom brought dog tags and military bracelets for the whole class, and I got to pass them out to everyone. We sang her two patriotic songs, and one of my classmates even played her a song on the violin. I felt proud of my mom. It was cool to be the center of attention. Mom stayed for a couple hours, and after that, we went back to our normal school day. I was happy I made that day happen before she left.

Chapter 13

YOU BETTER WATCH OUT

Christmas was coming the next weekend and I was so excited. But unfortunately, the night after Mom's party at school, I didn't feel good. We decided to not go to piano, but my mom and I still drove to Mrs. Garcia's house to drop off her Christmas present. We had bought her a piano ornament for her tree. My mom ran it in, and she said that Mrs. Garcia gave her a big hug and asked if her Sunday school class could send her some stuff while she was away. Mrs. Garcia was crying and told Mom that she would pray for her. I thought it was cool that someone who wasn't even in our family was going to do something nice for my mom.

We went home and laid low for the rest of the night. Then, at 3:30 a.m., I woke up not feeling good at all. I started screaming for my mom and dad. They got into my room just in time to see me throwing up all over my bed. I felt absolutely terrible! I couldn't breathe very well. My mom and dad kept telling me to calm down and said everything was OK. They cleaned up me and the bed and had me lay down on the sofa in the living room.

My mom stayed home with me the next day because she was done working at Franklin Energy to prepare for her deployment. I thought having my mom with me was the best because this would be the last time for seven months that she could stay home all day. I think I threw up seven times that day. Even though it sucked being sick, having time with my mom made me feel good inside. I started to feel better the next day, which was awesome because I wanted to be better by Christmas. I thought I could do it.

Then Christmas Eve came! We went to Aunt Deb's house in Fond du Lac, Wisconsin. I got to play with my second cousin, Dustin. Aunt Deb has four cats, and one of them is mean. Dustin and I tried to find him, but my uncle told us to leave him alone. My aunts gave my mom a lot of stuff because she was leaving for her deployment, and they had even put up a tree that was red, white, and blue. Aunt Lori made a big wooden sign that talked about being brave. It was a fun night, but I was more excited about Christmas morning. I couldn't wait to open all my presents at home.

On Christmas morning, my mom and dad woke me up and I went running downstairs. We handed out all the gifts, and I ended up having the most. I had probably fifteen gifts in total. My mom made Dad and me open a few gifts together. The first one I opened was a huge box. There was a big teddy bear in there holding a sign that said the bear would snuggle with me while Mom was gone. This was so I could feel like I had her with me while she was gone. Then my mom had my dad open a box that had perfume in it so he could smell her scent while she was gone. The third package had two little voice recorders with messages from my mom. One was for my dad and one was for me. She said this way we could hear her while she was gone. Mine was to say goodnight to me every night. My mom said there was one more package that didn't come yet, and it was a big cardboard cutout of her in uniform. This was for my dad and me to see her while she was gone. I opened the rest of my presents and I got almost everything on my Christmas list. I told Mom and Dad that it was one of the best Christmases ever!

At 11:30 a.m. on Christmas day, we went to Aunt Sue's house for Christmas brunch and to open presents with all of my dad's family. My cousin had his PlayStation up and I got to play it. The games were *Dirt Rally*, *Dirt Four*, *Project Cars 2*, and *Forza Motorsports 7*. It was cool because he had a steering wheel I could use. I only had a controller at home. I drove well except for *Dirt Rally*. I kept flipping the car over and driving off the cliffs.

After that, we went to my grandma and grandpa's house to open more presents. I got a twenty-pack of Hot Wheels, football cards, a football, and some lottery tickets.

That night when Mom was putting me to bed, I started crying again because she was leaving in a week. I said that there was nothing to look forward to anymore because Christmas was over. I couldn't stop crying for a while. I asked her if I could get up to blow my nose and go downstairs to give Dad a hug. I just wanted to have my dad be a part of it too. There is something with me and my family where we always want the three of us to be together. It was really going to be hard with my mom gone. It was supposed to be the three of us together, and that wasn't going to happen for seven months. I was sad about that.

Chapter 14

THE FLU AND OVERHEATING

During the week between Christmas and New Year's, my mom got the flu. I am 95% sure it was from me the week before. When I woke up, my dad told me that Mom wasn't feeling good. He said she needed to stay home for the day. With Mom being sick, it felt like it was practice for Dad and me because even though she was here, we wouldn't see her for the day. I came in to check on her before we left for Kids Inc. It made me feel bad because she didn't look good. I refilled her water glass for her. We didn't hug because we didn't want to keep passing the flu to each other.

When Dad and I left, we had to take the rental car because Mom's car was in the repair shop. Her windshield washer sprayer was not working. It turned out that a few other things needed to be fixed on her car, too, because the mechanic had screwed up. The rental car was a BMW. The car was black with flecks in the paint. The interior was tan leather. I have to say that I liked it a lot. We have always been a family that loves cars. On the way to Kids Inc., it said on the dashboard that the engine was overheating. Dad dropped me off. Later that night, he told me that the engine temperature got up to 250 degrees. Dad had to take the car in to get a different one.

Mom still wasn't feeling the best, but she had to go out to her base for final stuff in preparation for her deployment. She brought home a ton of things, like folders, papers, gas mask filters, et cetera. She had so much stuff to pack and send to the Middle East. She was also told that she needed to fly out a day early. She would now be leaving on New Year's Day at 0700. I felt terrible that she wasn't going to be able to spend the entire New Year's Day with us.

I knew that I had not been the best helper during the past week. I had felt a bunch of bad emotions in my head every day. I tried to crush them up and throw them away, but that didn't work. I felt like I took it out on my family because I didn't know how to stop thinking about it.

That same week, we also took down all the Christmas decorations. My mom was trying to help Dad and me as much as possible, so we worked together and got it done before she left. Dad kept on saying that if Mom didn't help us, the decorations might be up until July when she got back home. I felt sad about this, too, because every other year we had left the decorations up for a little longer. I didn't think the house felt right when the decorations were down. The warmth and sparkle were gone. Everything started to feel strange.

Two days before Mom left, she gave me one last present. It was a Lego set. There was a note on the box. It said that I should put one piece on every day while she was gone. When she came home, we would put the last pieces on so we could play with it. It was a military tank and there were 221 pieces to the set. I thought it was a cool way to count down to her return.

It seemed like over 200 days was a long time! It would be hard for Dad and me to be without her for so long, but we would have to figure it out. Dad was sad that week, too.

Chapter 15

WEEK 1: IT'S REALLY HAPPENING

We left for the airport at 4:45 a.m. on the day Mom deployed. I knew it was going to be a terrible day. I remember waking up early to the sound of Mom packing her stuff into her backpack. I had to get dressed and eat some breakfast. It went so fast. Next thing I knew, we were in the car on the way to the airport. After we checked in, we met up with some of her coworkers from the base before getting to the gate. One of the people was a girl who was flying with Mom, and another was a man who had his uniform on. Some people were coming up to him and thanking him for protecting our country. It made me feel good that my mom was part of that.

After a little bit, we went with my mom to go down to her gate. We had to go through security first, though, but it wasn't a problem. We got to go with Mom to the gate because she was in the military. Otherwise, we would have had to say goodbye to her at the security checkpoint. We hung together as a family for a while and talked about fun things from the holidays. I could tell that Mom and Dad were trying to be happy for me. When Dad and I were walking away, Mom took a secret picture of us. I didn't know about the picture until Dad told me later that day.

When we were on the way home, Mom sent a text saying her flight was being delayed six hours. While we were still driving, she called Dad and asked him to set up a Netflix account for her so she could watch TV while she was waiting.

When we got home, I needed to take care of Bear's food, water, and litter box. As I was coming up the stairs, Bear cut in front of me and made me bang into a picture on the wall. It bounced on the step and down the rest of the stairs, ending up in pieces. It scared the crap out of me. I started crying and Dad came over to say it was OK. Turns out Mom wanted to change something in the picture anyway, so that made me feel a little better about it.

The rest of the day, Dad and I didn't really do much. Nothing felt right. Dad went grocery shopping later that afternoon, and I stayed home and played on my Xbox. Mom called a while later and said that she was finally leaving and wouldn't get to Norfolk until almost midnight. She spent the entire day at the airport. Crazy!

The next day was Tuesday, and I was a little slow waking up because I had to get up at my normal time, 6:00 a.m. I was not able to sleep in like I had during Christmas break. I had Kids Inc. and it felt like a normal day. We didn't do much because it was too cold to go outside. My dad picked me up to go to my workout with Luke, the trainer. Dad worked out with me for a while but he had to stop to help Mom with her phone issues when she called him. He was able to join us after a little bit. The workout was fun. Luke always had something new for me to do.

After working out, we had to go to the orthodontist. Dr. Daub had to measure my jaw movement, and then I had new bands put on my braces. I changed the color from blue to black. Dad had mentioned that I might get my headgear that day, but it turns out that I didn't. I felt like jumping up and down 50,000 times! I was not looking forward to wearing the headgear, so the longer I got to wait, the better. It turned out that it would be another month before I got the headgear. The only thing I had to do for now was have Dad adjust the bracket on my teeth four more times.

That night at bedtime, Dad and I each played our recorded messages that Mom made for us. When I played my message, my mom had made it so that I could say stuff in between her words, which is just like what we would do every night when she was here. I thought it was very neat that I have a mom who came up with all these ideas. She seemed to always be thinking of ways to make things special for me.

I woke up the next morning for my first day back to school since Christmas break. I got to see my classmates for the first time in a couple weeks, and this made me happy. I also found out that I had to take a math test I missed when I was sick. It went well!

In my class, we counted down the days on a whiteboard until my mom got home. Mrs. Halleen changed the number each day. We started that day. None of my classmates asked me any questions or said anything about my mom. That was OK, though, because I didn't want anyone to bring it up. It would have made me sad!

I had piano on Thursday night and it went well. Mrs. Garcia was asking some questions about Mom. She asked if she could have my mom's mailing address to send her something.

That week felt strange. It seemed like Dad and I were just going about our lives as usual, but Mom was traveling to the other side of the globe to protect our country. Life just kept going.

On Saturday, it felt like a normal Guard weekend for me because we don't really see Mom much during the day on those weekends, only at night. We still couldn't go outside because it had been near or below zero for a week. I did have a swim lesson that day. The instructor scheduled two people at the same time, so Dad and I got to play around for a while until the instructor was done with the other person.

That night Mom FaceTimed us. She was finally in Qatar. It was nuts to think about how long it took to travel there. I was so excited to see her on the phone. We got to see her room and some of the buildings outside. It was dark, so we couldn't see too much. Mom seemed tired and sad. She didn't seem like herself. I couldn't even imagine how she must have been feeling.

The next day, Dad and I were home all day and watched football. It didn't feel the same because normally we would have one of the TVs on a channel Mom liked and we would put football on the other two, usually the Packers and NFL RedZone. It felt odd without Mom there.

Sometimes Dad and I would talk about the TV shows Mom used to watch, like decorating or fix-it-up shows. We would talk about if we liked the house or some of the things they did to fix it up. Without Mom, we now had two TVs on football and one on Xbox.

When I played Xbox, I tried to make some friends. I could go online, free roam, and click a button to join a session if I was lucky. I had been finding other players online, and I could talk to them and hear what they said. That way, I had more people to talk to. Dad was sometimes busy with stuff around the house, so he wasn't always there to talk with.

Chapter 16

WEEK 2:
THE EXPERIMENT

On Monday, we started an experiment to see how parent pick-up would be. Instead of going to Kids Inc. at 3:45 p.m. when school let out, Dad picked me up and took me home. That way I didn't overload with staying at Kids Inc. until suppertime each night. Dad would leave to go to the gym and my responsibility was to get my homework done, which usually took less than an hour. It felt odd because it was something new and I wasn't used to going home that early.

The first time we did parent pick-up experiment, I called Dad shortly after he left and said it sounded like somebody was shoveling outside. I was kind of scared being home alone. It ended up being some construction from across the street. I was relieved when Dad told me what he'd seen when he was leaving. It felt good to just be home and take more responsibility for myself. I finished all my homework and got to have some free time on my phone watching some videos until Dad got back. We ate supper and we talked about how it had gone. Then he checked all my homework to make sure it was correct and signed my sheets for my teacher. It felt good to get it right the first time. The next chance to try parent pick-up would be on Friday.

Mom called Monday night and we were able to talk about how parent pick-up had gone that day. She said she was proud of me for doing a good job and owning it. It makes me feel good about myself when she says she is proud of me. If she's proud of me, then I'm proud of myself. And that's a pretty cool feeling.

The next couple of days were busy with working out, swimming, and piano lessons. On each of those nights, I still had to get my homework done, so it was a lot of work. The nights went by fast and there was not much free time for Xbox or my phone.

We were able to talk to Mom each night, which felt good. With her being able to FaceTime us, it was better than just a normal phone call. She had moved into her permanent building on Wednesday. She showed us her room and the common area outside of her room. It looked like a jail with all the rooms around the outside and tables and stuff in the middle. I was happy for her because she could finally unpack her boxes and the crate with her stuff in it. I hoped that would help her feel better about the deployment and being gone.

Each night, I added one Lego piece to the Humvee 3000. At the end of the second week, it had four wheels and fourteen total pieces put together.

We had to sign up for parent pick-up for the next week. We were going to try and do the same thing we'd already done, where I would come home right after school on Monday and Friday. I was excited to keep doing this. One of the first things Mom had said to me when she called was that I needed to be a big boy and do some stuff on my own. This was one way to do that.

On Saturday morning, I had to take care of Bear's food, water, and litter box before I could play with my games or phone. That night, I had my best friend Sam over to my house for a sleepover again. We had a chance to play Madden 18 online with my friend Mali. That night, Mom called while Sam was here. We all had a chance to talk to her. It's always good to talk with Mom, even with Sam there. She asked him how he was doing, too. With Sam over, it helped keep my mind busy with games and watching videos on our phones. Having him over was a good thing because I didn't think about Mom as much as normal.

After Sam left on Sunday, I was tired from staying up until about midnight. I wasn't very motivated. But I didn't really have to do much except feed and take care of Bear, which I was happy for.

Chapter 17

WEEK 3: GREEN LIGHT BULBS

The next day was Monday, and I was still tired. It was week two of our parent pick-up experiment. I had my homework all done when Dad got home. He wanted me to journal that night, so it was important that I got my other stuff done. It had been over two weeks since Mom deployed. The time felt like it was crawling along. It just seemed like it was going to take forever for Mom to get home.

On Tuesday, Dad told me after our workout that he had talked to my teacher about making a Valentine's Day project with all my classmates, and we could send it to Mom as a present. I thought it was a pretty cool idea and just another way to show that other people, even my classmates, loved and cared for her. Dad also stopped at the post office to send Mom a care package with snacks, magazines, and a Rubik's Cube. Mom told us that there was a guy in Qatar with her that knew how to solve it, and he was going to teach her. I hoped she would figure it out and could come home and show me.

We didn't talk to Mom for a couple days. It was Wednesday night when we got to connect. I wished we could talk every day, but she had been really busy. When we did talk, she mentioned that she was training soldiers from other countries like England and Germany. That made me feel proud because it sounded like it was important and that she was doing some high-level stuff. I can't even imagine all the jobs she was doing. I tried to picture it, but it was hard. I felt lonely with her gone.

The next day, after school and piano, my dad mentioned that he was contacting all the relatives who got a green lightbulb from us as Christmas presents. People use green lights to show their support for soldiers and to show they're thinking of them. We wanted everyone to put the green bulb in a porch light at their house and leave it on until my mom came home safely. Dad was hoping that everyone would send selfies with the green light lit in their yard. He was talking to Aunt Lori (my godmother) about it, hoping she could help call people, too. If she could reach out to everyone on Mom's side of the family, we would text everyone on Dad's side to do it too. The first person to send something back was Aunt Sue with a picture of her and my cousin Austin. Then, over the next couple of days, my cousin Alex (who lives in Denver), Eric, and Uncle John all sent their pictures. I thought it was cool that the family was sending their pictures. I texted our neighbor Erin because she'd had her green light on since Christmas, and I told her, "Thanks for rockin' the green light." My dad and I took a picture as well to send to Mom. All those green lights were turned on for my mom and wouldn't be turned off until she was home. It was very special to see.

On Saturday, we got an email from Mom saying she was feeling sad because she missed us. I felt so bad for her so we called her as soon as we could. After the call, Dad and I started talking about trying to cheer her up. So, we put our plan into action. We sent the picture of Aunt Sue with my cousin Austin, and another selfie with my Uncle John and a sign that said, "Make America Great Again." Once she received the texts, she replied and said they made her feel better. She also said she cried a little because she knew people were thinking of her. We texted my aunt to say thank you for Mom and let her know the pictures helped.

Later that morning, I was kind of singing a song when Dad asked me about helping on another idea for making Mom feel better. He said he had a song on his phone that was heavy metal but had good words in it. We talked about what it meant and that it had a good meaning. Dad went to the internet and found all the words in the song to show me what it was saying. When he read the words to me, he started to tear up. It meant more than I expected a song like that would. It was basically saying that you shouldn't be the person who fades away when you face challenges. But instead, you should be the person who rises and takes your shot at overcoming the challenge.

It seemed like Mom, Dad, and I were all going through what this song was talking about. It was hard, but we were all going through this together and it was our first time. Dad sent an email to Mom with all the lyrics in it. She said she could see me singing the song. It motivated her to push through, and it was perfect for what she needed at that time. I felt a lot better and knew that she was going to be tough.

I knew Mom was struggling a little being so far from home. One night when we were talking with her, Dad mentioned about being "Semotan Strong" at the end of the phone call. (Our last name is Semotan.) I liked it. It meant we had to be tough through the hard times, all of us. Maybe a week later, Mom said she was out near a B-52 bomber plane that had bombs hanging under it. She got up next to one of the bombs and wrote "Semotan Strong" on it. These bombs would be dropped in enemy territory soon. I thought that was amazing. Some bad people got killed when they were used. I told her if she had another chance to write on a bomb, she should write "9/11 This" on it.

I was lucky because I was able to talk to Mom almost every day during the third week of her deployment. It felt good because seeing her was like she was in the room with me for a little while each day. One morning, Dad checked to see how much the phone bill was going to be and he thought it looked like it was going to be our normal charges. Then, a day later, we got the bill and it was over $700.00. I knew we had been talking to Mom a lot, but this was like, WOW! I immediately worried that we would not be able to talk to Mom as much. That made me feel terribly bad.

Dad went to the phone store that same day to talk to the people there about it. They gave us some ideas and took some money off our bill, which was nice of them. After that, it didn't cost anything to talk or see her, but sometimes we lost the connection because everything was being done through Wi-Fi. At least we could talk for free after that. That was the most important thing!

Chapter 18

WEEK 4: VALENTINE'S DAY CARDS

It was coming up on a month that Mom had been gone already. It seemed like the time went both fast and slow for me. I know I said that before, but it continued to be a strange feeling. We only had about five more months of deployment to go. My weeks were steady with school, working out, swimming, and piano lessons. The weekends went fast since my friend Sam stayed at my house one time and I was at his house another weekend because my dad had to work.

Dad and I had been spending lots of time planning things or items to send Mom to make sure she had snacks and some stuff from home. Dad mentioned that Mom got a package from people she works with. I thought it was cool that the people from her work cared about her and were sending her things. That probably made her very happy.

It was Kindness Week at school, which meant that every day we had to do something for our community or others. On

Friday, we made special Valentine's cards for Mom to show her that my classmates cared and had love for her. It made me feel good that everyone was doing something kind for her. I have twenty-six classmates, the largest class in the school, so we had a lot of Valentines to send. Around that time, it seemed like a lot of my classmates were asking me how Mom was doing. I usually told them that it was going OK, but time was going by slowly. It seemed to come and go with my classmates. They would ask questions and then seem to forget about it. I wouldn't forget about it, though. It was on my mind every day.

Dad and I made another care package for Mom. We wanted to make sure that she got the Valentine's cards from my class in time. Also, in the package to go to Mom, we sent a wood plaque. Dad asked a guy he works with to make a special plaque out of wood for her. It said "Semotan Strong" on it along with "Qatar," the year, and the Air Force logo. I thought it was very cool that someone took the time to make it for her. The guy who made it didn't even know my mom, but he wanted to help anyway. We had a whole bunch of other stuff that was in the package, too, including a picture frame we have at home, snacks, toilet paper, and a magazine. We thought she would get the package a day or two before Valentine's Day. Dad also picked up two packs of Valentine's cards for Mom to give out over there. She said there were some people that she wanted to give them to so they would feel good, too. It was neat that she was thinking of other people. When we talked with her, she said she was trying to send something to us in time for Valentine's Day, too! It was always exciting to see what she sent!

It had been an awesome week. Everything felt like it was going my way. In class, my teacher had a program where people could earn or lose points. When students got twenty points or more, they got to have lunch with the teacher. I got to have lunch two days in a row with my teacher, along with my friend Ethan. My teacher told Ethan and me that we are two of only eight kids to have ever done that in her thirteen years of teaching. It seemed like it was a good week for everybody in my class for some reason. At least one person every day received ten points.

We also had an open house at school that week. An open house is when family members or guardians can come into our classroom and see all the work we are doing. My teacher set up a scavenger hunt in the classroom for the parents to do with us. It made me feel good that I could show my work to my dad. I like to see how proud he is of me with everything going on. I was showing him some of my work, which included a Wisconsinite Report on our governor. I also showed him how to build an electric current with a battery and lightbulb. Another thing we did was go into the music room and the Words Their Way classroom so I could introduce him to my other teachers. It was different with Mom not being there, though. Nothing felt the same.

Before the open house, I had a piano lesson. The lesson went well and Mrs. Garcia scored me an eight. That week, I worked harder on piano because my mom wanted to watch me play during one of her calls with us. Later that night, when she was on the FaceTime call, she watched me play the song "America" on the keyboard. She said it sounded like the best thing she ever heard. That made my night. Mom told us that she received a card from Mrs. Garcia that week, too. She asked me to thank her at my next piano lesson. It made me feel good that so many people were showing how much they cared about her while she was away. Some of the people, like the guy who made the plaque, didn't even know her. It just surprises me when people do nice things for others that they don't know.

At swim lessons on Wednesday, Dad wanted to take a video of me swimming to show Mom before my lessons were done. Once I could swim a lap of the pool good enough for my instructor, I would graduate. It was going OK that night, but Dad just wanted me to work on getting my kicks stronger. I did the swim for him and he recorded it. I must have done great because my coach said, "Yeah, just like that!" Dad asked why I did better that time, and I told him I had just tried harder. In my head, I was thinking that maybe it was because I knew he was showing it to Mom. I wanted to make her happy. I learned if I just pushed myself a bit harder, I seem to do better.

Chapter 19

WEEKS 5 & 6:
SUNSHINE PACKAGES
& STRAY CATS

While Dad and I were journaling, Mom sent some pictures from Qatar. It was crazy to see what it looks like there. Just seeing the pictures made me feel like I was there with her and knew what she saw every day. It looked like it was hot and dry with lots of sand and desert. There were not very many buildings outside of the base. One picture was of the brick building she was staying in. It did not look too exciting. Very plain and boring.

She also sent a picture of a kitten that followed her back to her building. She said it meowed all the way as she walked. I thought the cat was cute. She says there are lots of cats begging for food. The soldiers are not supposed to feed them, though. Mom said that the cats were there to control the mice and rat population, and if the soldiers feed them, the cats will not be hungry enough to kill the mice. Also, she said that none of the cats are treated by a vet, so they could have diseases. She said that she was told about several soldiers breaking the rules and feeding them anyway.

At that point, my mom had been gone for six weeks. Looking back, it still felt like it was going so slowly. That week, Dad and I noticed that one of our neighbors, who we hadn't even met yet, had started leaving a green light on in their backyard. We could see it from our living room window. Dad and I thought it was cool somebody we didn't even know was thinking of Mom. Dad took a picture and sent it to her saying somebody else was thinking of her. What I noticed is that lots of people come together during things like deployments.

That same week, we received the Valentine's package from Mom. Some of the things she sent were a stuffed camel wearing a hat and T-shirts for Dad and me that had "Al Udeid Air Force Base" written on them with the US flag. There was also some Arabic candy. The candy wrappers had a different kind of writing on the package. It was like nothing I had ever seen before. There was also some money from Qatar, and instead of dollars, it was called "riyal." Each bill had a different design. There were three types of birds on one, some crossed swords on another, and a sailboat on the water on the last one. There were no presidents like we have on our American dollars. There were also some stickers, hand-written letters for us, and two more recordings that we could listen to. One was for Dad for their anniversary and one was for me for my birthday. Also, Mom sent some Valentine's cards for Dad and me, too. And finally, there were some clothes and boots she wasn't going to need any longer because she had enough over there to wear. Man, she thought of everything. That package had a lot of stuff in it. I hoped she would get ours in time.

We heard from Aunt Lori, and she said she was sending a package of sunshine to Mom. That's what she called it. I wasn't sure what that meant, but I knew it would be fun if

Aunt Lori was doing it. She was sending it in the next couple of days. Mom would have plenty of packages from home arriving around Valentine's Day. I thought it would make her feel good that people were thinking of her.

I was getting a little worried that she still hadn't received the package with all the Valentine's cards from me, my classmates, and my dad. It was important to me that she got it in time for the holiday. When we asked about it during a call with her, she said so much mail came every day that it took a while to get it all sorted out. I just worried she would feel bad if it was late.

The big news the following week was that Dad and I might be able to go see her! Mom and Dad talked about Mother's Day weekend. Mom was trying to earn a four-day pass for her hard work. If she was able to get that, we could go to Qatar for four days! That sounded awesome to me!!! I knew it would probably be the best Mother's Day present ever!

My mom said it would be an eighteen- to twenty-hour flight! I thought it would be weird being in a plane that long, but I would do anything to go see my mom. Dad looked at some flights and hotels to stay at in the capital of Qatar, which is called Doha. Along the way, we would have a layover, most likely in Europe somewhere, and then fly to Doha. I saw some pictures of the hotels we could be staying at and they were very luxurious. Some were even right on the beach, which is the Persian Gulf.

Dad and I talked about the war that took place about twenty-five years ago in that area. We looked at some pictures that were taken during the war. Seeing pictures from then till now, it looks way different. Mom and Dad were going to keep talking about the trip. I prayed every night that it would happen.

Chapter 20

WEEK 7: HAWAIIAN SHIRTS

Each weekend, Dad sent Mom another picture of family members next to the green lights that we gave out as Christmas gifts. During her seventh week of deployment, it was Nana and Papa out in their front yard next to the light when it was snowing one day. Nana made a sign that said, "Thank you for your service and be safe." I think it was a good idea that Dad had them take pictures and sent them to Mom to let her know that the family members were still thinking of her all the time. My dad tried to do so many things to make sure Mom was happy and knew people were thinking of her.

That weekend, Dad also told me the trip was confirmed. Mom received the four-day pass and he finished the reservations for the trip to Doha. We wouldn't go until May, but I was already so excited and nervous. I was wondering if it was going to be safe for Dad and me. I was also thinking about all the time in a plane and just what it would be like over there. A couple months later, I would know.

It was the weekend for decisions because we also decided where my birthday party in March was going to be. Dad had been spending a lot of his free time doing all this planning for me, and I felt kind of bad that he had to do it all. I really appreciated it, though. We decided it was going to be at Lasertag Adventure. I had been there before and really liked it. Dad even folded the invitations for the party before I woke up one morning. Those were things my mom had always done, so I knew he was doing A LOT for me with Mom gone. I could see he was sad, though. He and Mom always did so much together that I was sure he was lonely at times, too.

On Monday of that week, Mom finally received our Valentine's package we sent. She said she also got the one from Aunt Lori, too. She called Dad at work earlier that day when she saw the plaque he had made. She really loved it. She was so excited for all the Valentine's cards from my classmates. She was the most surprised about the cards. Making her feel good made me feel good. She even got everything in time! Success!

Wednesday was Valentine's Day and Dad and I each wore our new shirts that Mom had sent. It felt good to wear a shirt that came all the way from an Air Force base in Qatar. It felt like we had a piece of her with us all day. We took a selfie and sent it to her before leaving for school and work. That night, I had my last swim lesson and Dad recorded another video to show Mom. She was even more proud of me finishing the lessons and being able to swim two different kinds of strokes. I felt good about being able to swim two of the four kinds of strokes. The harder ones, I wasn't going to learn any time soon. But I was OK with accomplishing what I did.

One night, Dad saw an article in the paper about a bad person being killed by a drone overseas. When he asked Mom about it, she said, "You're welcome." I guess he was not a very nice person and was someone who they were looking for. I was happy and proud of her at the same time. My mom got to know about so much stuff in the military that I couldn't even imagine. I tried sometimes, but it all seemed so big and important. I knew she couldn't tell everything she was doing while she was there. I couldn't wait to hear about more stuff when she came home.

In my class, there was a boy named Alex. His mom talked to my teacher and Dad about sending some Hawaiian shirts to Mom's squadron overseas. I thought it would look kind of funny with a bunch of soldiers wearing these shirts, but if it made them not think about where they were, then I was all for it. I hoped it would work out.

Later that night when I talked to Mom, I got sad on the phone with her because she wasn't going to be there for my birthday. I was turning double digits (I was going to be ten) and she wouldn't be there to celebrate. She felt bad about not being there, and we each cried a little. She had an idea, though. She suggested that we do a ten-and-a-half-year birthday party in September. That would be different, but at least we could all celebrate together as a family. I liked the idea, especially since I could get two parties out of it.

On Friday of that week, Dad and I wore our "RED" Friday shirts, which stands for "Remember Everyone Deployed." The shirts are red and have the US flag on them. Mine has a soldier saluting. At the rec department, Miss Candace, one of the instructors, asked me what "RED" means, and I told her. I liked that she asked what it stood for. She thought it was a good idea to have something that makes us think about the people who are deployed.

Part of getting ready for the trip to see Mom was getting my first passport. Dad had to do lots of paperwork. We went to the post office, where we filled out the application. He told me that I had to get my picture taken before we could order the passport. The picture part went OK. I hate pictures, but it was over quickly. Mom also needed to do some paperwork over in Qatar and mail it to us before we could do anything else. We were one step closer to being able to go see Mom.

Chapter 21

WEEK 8:
WHY AM I SICK AGAIN?

It was my family's annual tradition to go to Longboat Key, Florida every February. I only had my piano lesson and one day of school before we left! Yes!

The piano lesson went well, but after I fell asleep that night, I woke up not feeling good and yelled for Dad. I knew I was going to throw up! I told him to bring the bowl we use, but Dad got back too late. I ended up getting sick all over the bedspread and sheets. It tasted awful! Dad was running around cleaning and making sure it didn't get on the carpet, and I don't think it did. Then, the next thing I knew, I was climbing down from my bed and going into the bathroom to kneel by the toilet. It was like 1:00 in the morning and I couldn't stop throwing up.

I guessed I wasn't going to school the next day (Friday). We had a presentation day for a project I had been working on with classmates. But worse yet, we were supposed to be leaving for Florida on Saturday morning. I had no idea how I was going to feel going through airports and flying. The last thing

I remember was that Dad wanted me to go back to bed, and it was 3:00 in the morning. Dad had to wash all the bedding while I slept on the couch.

The next morning, Nana came over to watch me for a while so Dad could go to work. When he got home, I still wasn't feeling the best. I slept for most of the day. I hardly knew Nana was even there.

Saturday morning came and Dad and I left for the airport. I still was tired and weak, so I was lying down on the chairs in the airport until it was time to get on the plane. When we got to Chicago, I was feeling a little better and Dad wanted me to eat something. Hoping I was over the flu, we gave it a try. We went to the McDonald's in the airport and Dad got me two hash browns. I started feeling better almost before I finished the second one. Dad took a picture and sent it to Mom with me smiling and holding a hash brown in my hand, letting her know I was doing better.

The next flight took us to Florida! I couldn't wait! We were going to be in our new condo for the first time that year. It was cool that we had our own place but could still see all the rest of our family members, who were staying just two doors away. Since Mom was not there that year, Dad slept in my room with me. It was kind of cool to share a room since we'd never really done that before. It was like having company and hanging out with a friend, I guess.

The next couple of days, we spent most of the time in the swimming pool, on the beach, and playing tennis at night with the entire family. There were ten of us there so we had lots of teams. Even Papa played for a little bit, which was nice since he was like almost eighty years old.

It felt empty in our condo because Mom was not there in Florida. Things like her thoughtfulness and her just being there were missing for me. When you're used to three people doing things and then there are two, it just feels different. Like a missing puzzle piece. One good thing was that we were able to talk to her each night before bedtime, just like at home. We could tell her about what we did each day and find out how her day went. We sent some pictures from the new condo. There was one with me and her cardboard cutout sitting on the balcony chairs, and one of me and the cutout standing with the ocean behind us. She loved that Dad and I brought her cardboard cutout with us. We said we wanted it to feel like she was here.

Dad let me stay up later each night to watch some street racing and car shows on TV. It felt fun—just Dad and I hanging out like two guys and enjoying the same shows before bed.

During the day, we would go and hang out at the beach with my cousins. I played baseball with one of my older cousins, Eric. Dad said Eric had played baseball for a long time, and he had watched Eric play when he was my age. In Florida, Eric taught me a little. He said my pitching was pretty good, which made me feel proud. I also spent lots of time in the pool with Dad playing catch or "chicken fights." Chicken fights are two people sitting in inner tubes and trying to tip each other over. Whoever is left floating is the winner. You can use your arms or legs, whatever you need.

Every night in Florida, we had something different for supper. My favorite night was when we went out for pizza and I ate eight slices. Dad took a picture of me and sent it to Mom. She couldn't believe I ate that much. We tried to take lots of pictures to keep Mom informed, but they were also for the calendar she makes each year. On one of the nights, we took our family picture on the beach. We took the cardboard cutout of Mom to the beach to take the picture with everyone wearing camouflage. Dad had bought all of us camouflage hoodies or T-shirts to wear. I thought they were awesome. The whole family wore them to support Mom. We took two pictures. The first one was a regular one with everyone smiling and the second one was a serious look with our arms crossed, trying to look mean. It was fun. Mom thought the pictures were neat.

On Saturday, at the end of the week, we had to come home to Wisconsin and the cold hit us hard. We were happy to be home, though. We come back on Saturday every year so we can go to the new car show on Sunday. I enjoy going to the show. It has always been one of my favorite things. I love to see all the new, fancy, and high-tech cars for the new year. My favorite was the Lamborghini Aventador. Dad took pictures again for the calendar and to send Mom. It seemed like he was turning into Mom with all the pictures he was taking (ha-ha). He also let me buy two Jada cars. That made me start thinking about my birthday, which was about eight days away.

Chapter 22

WEEK 9:
WE ESCAPED

A new week was starting, but we didn't have school on Monday. That was all right with me because I wasn't ready to go back. It is always hard after you come back from vacation. I did have basketball practice starting Monday night, though. It went well for the first night, but Dad couldn't stay to watch. He had a Little League meeting to attend since I was going to play baseball that year for the first time.

I was a little worried about baseball because it was all new to me. I thought that some people out there would be way better because they had been playing for a long time. But Dad told me that it's not the big leagues and my chances of getting hurt were almost zero. That helped me feel better. I also worried about other kids saying things to me. I didn't want kids yelling at me if I messed up on a play or something. Dad and I talked about this too and he said that everyone makes mistakes. If I made some in my first year, it would be OK. It was brand new to me, so I was just a little anxious and excited at the same time. It was times like that when I missed Mom because she had always helped me with my nerves.

My birthday was less than a week away, so that was all I had been thinking about. Everyone had been asking me what I wanted for my birthday. I kept saying that Xbox gift cards, iTunes cards, or Jada cars (like the ones I got at the car show) were all I wanted. Dad had been working on planning my party and inviting my friends. I invited about ten friends in total. We hadn't been hearing back from their parents if they could come or not. This made me a little concerned. If no one came to my party, I would have been so sad. Mom had said on the phone that seven to eight of my friends would be a good number. Otherwise, she said, I couldn't really hang out or see all of them because there would be so many. She always knew the right things to say to make me feel better.

On Saturday, my dad had to work so Nana came over in the morning to watch me until he got home. We went out for breakfast and then went shopping. I thought it was nice that Nana helped out with Mom being gone. We went to McDonald's and then went to Target for my birthday presents. I ended up getting three more Jada cars to add to the ones I got at the car show. I got five cars in one week. That was awesome! My birthday was coming up in two days. I thought, "Who knows? Maybe I'll get more."

On Sunday afternoon, Aunt Sue took Dad and me to a place called Breakout Games. Nana, Papa, some of my cousins, and my uncle were also there. It was super cool because it was one of those places where you had to figure out how to escape from a room. The theme of the room was about a bunch of kidnappings. You had to figure out the sequence to escape before a bad guy came for you. It was a lot of fun. Mom would have really liked it because she is good at figuring out the clues.

It was kind of weird with her not being there since she had done escape rooms before with Dad and me.

We were in the room for like an hour in total. We were blindfolded and handcuffed. First, we had to get ourselves out of the handcuffs before we could start searching the room for clues. We figured everything out with twenty-two seconds left. At the end, we had our pictures taken, and they were stamped with the time and the room name, "Kidnapped." We sent a picture to Mom when we talked that night. Before we talked to her, though, we all went to Taco Bell for dinner, which is one of my favorite places to eat. The whole afternoon was fun doing the Breakout Games with everyone. I hoped we could go back there someday with Mom to see if we could get out faster. During times like that, I really missed her. I wished she could have been there that night.

Chapter 23

WEEKS 9 & 10: GRIM23

The next day, Dad and I went out to eat at Pizza Hut. We got to eat for free because I had done enough reading each day over the previous couple of weeks to earn a free pizza coupon. Each day, we had to read thirty minutes and then record it on a sheet. My mom or dad needed to sign the sheet each day to make sure I did my reading. I enjoyed my reading because the books I picked were interesting and fun. Some were mysteries, some were from the *I Survived* series for kids, and one was from the *Diary of a Wimpy Kid* books. Dad read his own books with me sometimes when he wasn't doing other stuff. I liked it when we could read together. I felt like it was another way we could spend time together. Mom also started reading books while she was in Qatar. She was reading *Red Sparrow*. I thought maybe we could all read together when she got back.

Finally, my birthday party came! All my friends met me at Lasertag Adventure. Mom was right. I had eight of my friends come. We played laser tag and trampoline dodgeball. I thought it was awesome to have my friends there. Some I had known for a long time through football, and others were friends from school that I'd met that year. It was an awesome time. Dad's friend from work made the cupcakes and birthday cake. The cake had a hand grenade on top that was made from Rice Krispies and covered with green frosting.

We were there for over three hours. I wanted my dad to play laser tag, but he couldn't due to all the stuff he had to do for the party like hanging decorations. He did everything to make sure the party went well. I really appreciated what he did. Normally, Mom and Dad worked together to make sure it went well, but this time it was Dad making sure by himself. Mom had been saying on the phone and in some of the letters she sent that she really appreciated what he was doing. I did, too.

At the end of the party, before everyone left, we took a group picture. It was me and my friends standing by the cardboard cutout of Mom. We sent it to her later. She really liked the picture and was excited to see everyone who was there.

Sunday was really the last big thing for my birthday week with my friend Sam coming over for most of the day. We mostly just hung out and played some basketball, football, and Xbox. I liked the days when Sam and I could just hang.

Monday wasn't such a good day. Dad got upset with me because I wasn't helping in the morning and I got up later than normal. I had to be on time because Dad would have to work longer if he was late in the morning. If that happened, I wouldn't be able to do parent pick-up after school. We had talked about this a while ago, but for some reason, I wasn't doing my part. Dad had to make some rules about my phone and what would happen if I didn't get up and get ready on time. I would lose the phone one week for each minute I was late in the morning. I thought it was pretty harsh because sometimes I felt like we both screwed up in the mornings. But it seemed like I was the only one who would pay the price, not Dad. Dad had always asked me to take care of myself, and I needed to do better at that.

On Tuesday and for the rest of the week, I was up early, got my stuff done, and, as Dad says, I still had time to go on my phone. I felt good when I did the right things. If I stayed true to our agreement, then everything went great. I thought, "Hopefully, I can keep doing this and keep my phone." It wasn't really that hard to do, and it felt good keeping my word with Dad. Dad said each day, "Thanks, and I'm proud of you for helping."

A couple other big things that week were the Hoops Night basketball game at the high school and my classmate's mom sending the Hawaiian shirts to my mom. Dad and I bought some shirts and sent them to the lady who organized everything. She would be sending 120 shirts over to Mom and her troops in Qatar. Mom said they were going to have an event in April, and the shirts would arrive in time for that.

It was going to be a Hawaiian party, so the shirts would be perfect. I liked helping with sending these shirts because I knew Mom appreciated it. I got a good feeling about helping the soldiers have some fun while they were there.

On Friday night, I got to watch my teacher's basketball game against another school's teachers. The whole event was called Hoop-A-Looza. It was a lot of fun. Some of the kids showed their talents during breaks in the game or at halftime. The kids like me sat courtside on the floor and the parents were in the bleachers. All the kids signed each other's shirts with marker. We'd bought special shirts for the night with the Hoop-A-Looza logo and grade level for the number on the back. I got to see almost all my friends that night since nearly everyone came to the game. Dad sent a couple of pictures to Mom of some things that happened during the night.

On Saturday, some packages came in the mail. One of the packages was the last two Jada cars I ordered for my birthday gifts with the money Aunt Lori and Nana had given me. They were super cool. The other package was from my mom in Qatar. Inside it were some Easter cards for my dad and me, some Easter candy, Dad's birthday present (his birthday is in April), and some US flags.

The flags that Mom sent were signed by the pilots of one of the missions they went on in Afghanistan. I thought it was awesome that these flags had actually gone on a plane that flew a mission. All the flags were signed on the white edge of the flag by the members of the flight team. One flag came with a certificate that Mom got special for me. I planned on showing it in my bedroom somehow, maybe in a case or something. The pilot wrote on it, "Happy Birthday Jayden from GRIM23." There was also a safety pin from the bombs. This pin was pulled out when they released the bombs from the plane.

The candy that Mom sent was kind of weird. In Qatar, they have different kinds of Kit Kats that we don't even have here in America, like peanut butter or mint. Also, there were other candy bars that were shaped like little hippos. They were chocolate inside and out. They tasted good! We waited until the following weekend to open the Easter cards on the actual holiday. Dad's birthday wasn't until the end of the month, so he had to wait even longer to open his cards.

Mom got the package we sent her, too. We'd sent a bunch of stuff for Mom to give out as Easter presents to some of her troops. We sent plastic eggs that you can put candy in along with the candy, and a whole bunch of other things she needs for herself, like snacks, toothpaste, and bathroom stuff. We also shipped a big plastic bug to scare her as she opened the box and was digging for stuff.

Mom said that she also got the Hawaiian shirts. She opened one of the boxes and it was filled with snacks for her squadron. They really enjoyed it. It was one thing to send packages to Mom, but it was kind of weird sending packages to people I didn't even know. We did it because even though we didn't love them, we cared for them as people and wanted them to be happy. Some people might not even get packages from home, so it was a good feeling. Maybe "weird" isn't the right word, but it was just different thinking about someone besides my own family. I guess the big event wasn't happening for a couple weeks, but they were planning a luau with all the decorations. Mom said she would send some pictures.

Chapter 24

WEEK 11: EASTER

Wednesday was our first Little League practice and it went well. Everyone seemed to be cooperating with each other. The coach set up stations with hitting, fielding ground balls, and catching pop ups. I felt like I did a good job for my first ever practice. Dad said he was proud of me, and he also told Mom he was proud of me that night on the phone. After just one day, I was already looking forward to the next week's practice. Baseball seemed like it was going to be fun. Our first game wasn't for another month, so I needed to keep working at it.

Before we went to the next practice, we went out to eat. We picked one of the local restaurants because they have special donation nights. Dad and I picked one that would donate money to my Little League team for every dollar we spent on our food order. One promise I made to Mom before she left was to keep trying new foods. So, by going to this restaurant I was able to try a barbeque chicken wrap for the first time. It was a little messy but tasted pretty good. Also, at home Dad made me try steak, which was OK. One other new food I tried around that time was chocolate-covered pomegranates. They tasted mostly like chocolate with a little fruity taste. I decided I would eat them again if Dad bought more. I knew Mom would be happy that I was at least trying some other foods. I am keeping my promises to Mom!

Easter Break finally came. We had no school on Friday and the entire following week. We had a bunch of field trips scheduled for that week at Kids Inc. The zoo, a pizza factory, and a gymnastics place were all part of the activities for the week.

On Saturday, Dad and I decorated Easter eggs at home. Normally this was something that Mom took care of, but since she was gone, Dad and I did it. We decided to have her on a FaceTime call so she could be involved. It was a lot of fun because we had her cardboard cutout in the kitchen too. She was happy that she got to see us dying the eggs different colors while she was on the phone. We also sent her some pictures with me wearing some bunny ears and holding the colored eggs with her cardboard cutout behind me. Mom still wants to have lots of pictures, not only to see what's happening but also for the calendar she makes each year.

Sunday morning was Easter, and right after I got up, Mom called and said I was going to have an Easter egg hunt in the house since it was cold outside. It felt good that she could be present on the phone. Somehow, she knew where some of the eggs were hidden, along with my Easter basket. I knew Dad had told her a few things before she called just to mess with me a little bit. It was cool having her call from Qatar and be there for the entire egg hunt. I found all the eggs, including one that had a $10 bill in it and a golden egg that gave me a clue to a special present. It was a Lego car, and it was hidden in the drawer under my bed. There were a lot of pieces to the car, so I knew it would take Dad and me a long time to build.

We hoped to have it completed by the time Mom came home. We had Easter dinner at Nana's house later that day, but until then, we stayed home and relaxed.

All the family members were at Nana's house, including Aunt Sue and Uncle John's family. Nana had an Easter egg hunt just for me. She hid five eggs and five gifts. I found everything fast and got to snack on some of the Peeps that were gift-wrapped. It was fun because Nana made lots of snacks, including my favorite, meatballs. I had a bunch before supper and some more during supper as well. Everybody else ate ham and a bunch of other food that Dad said was really good. I took his word for it because it didn't look like anything I would like. It was a little bit odd not having Mom there, but she said she would call after we got home to see how it went. That would be Monday morning for Mom. Times like that made me feel sad for Mom being alone. She must have missed us, but she always seemed to worry about me more than herself.

Chapter 25

WEEK 12:
TIME TO "RANGER UP"

The week after Easter was my school's Spring Break, but more importantly, it was our first practice at the complex for baseball. This was where we would be for the rest of our practices and games. Dad dropped me off and stayed for a little while to watch. Once we were done warming up, he left and picked me up later. I didn't mind that he left. He had plenty to do with Mom being gone. Sometimes he went shopping, worked out, or just took care of stuff, I guess.

The week was fun with all the Kids Inc. field trips, but the thing I won't forget was my next baseball practice. I didn't feel good when I woke up. My throat hurt and I was tired. Worse yet, it was like twenty-two degrees outside, but practice wasn't canceled. Dad asked me to try my best to at least get through practice and then I could relax for the rest of the day. I ate the breakfast he asked me to and then took some medicine to at least help me feel a little better. We got to the field and it was freezing cold and windy. I warmed up with my friend Ethan, and then we started doing drills. Practice only lasted an hour, and I was glad it didn't go longer. It was so cold that it was hard to think about anything else. Dad left for a little bit and came back with hot chocolates for Ethan and me since we were giving him a ride home. The rest of the day, I didn't feel good. Dad said he was proud of me for "rangering up" to get through practice when I didn't feel good.

The rest of the weekend, I still felt sick. When it came time to go to school on Monday, there was no way I could go because my throat still hurt a lot. Dad had to call Nana to come and watch me so he could go to work. Normally Mom and Dad would split the day watching me, but with Mom gone, he had to call Nana. I appreciated her coming over but didn't talk much since my throat hurt. I mostly slept while she was at our house. She watched me until Dad came home to take me to the doctor. I don't really like going to the doctor, but it is worth knowing what's wrong. After we got home from the doctor's office, she called and said I had strep throat. I needed to be off of school another day. I had to have medicine for twenty-four hours before returning. Nana came back a second day to watch me.

I seemed to have been sick way more than usual that year. Not sure why? Maybe it had something to do with my mom being gone.

I finally got to go back to school on Wednesday, and the countdown board for Mom's return was at ninety-five days!

One of the nights when Mom called that week, I was really sad. I ended up taking the phone and hiding under the big teddy bear that she had given me for Christmas. I just felt like crying, and I wanted to have alone time with Mom. We talked for a bit, which made me feel better. I was never sure why the sadness would hit me, but when it came, there was just nothing I could do.

Chapter 26

WEEKS 13 & 14: SYRIA & THE BATTLE HYMN

The next week was a special week for all of us. It was the halfway point for Mom's deployment. It was good to know what that amount of time felt like. It had been just over three months that she'd been gone, so I had a feeling of what the next three months would feel like. Sometimes it felt like it was going 50 miles an hour and at other times it felt like it was going 1,000 miles per hour. The weeks and weekends were kind of mixed as far as being busy with time going fast and not busy, when I could just relax and play on my phone and Xbox.

It seemed like it was always busy for Dad between making meals, helping with homework, and just doing stuff around the house. I can't imagine what it felt like with all the stuff he had to do. Sometimes I just walked up to him and gave him a hug to say thanks because I appreciated what he was doing. In the past, it had been busy enough with both Mom and Dad around, but it seemed super busy with just him. He said he appreciated Mom's help, too. When it is the three of us, we can get things done faster so we have time to play games or do things as a family.

At the halfway point, I realized that we were just four weeks away from going to see Mom. I was thankful that she had earned the chance to leave the Air Force base so we could see each other. I was scared to go to Qatar but excited at the same time. I had my passport, finally. It came in the mail. My picture was very serious looking because you can't smile or have any expression. I kind of felt that I looked like a criminal.

Around the time that my passport came, there was another big event over where Mom is. When we talked on the phone one night, she mentioned that some things might be happening, and we would be able to read about it in the newspaper or see it on the news. There's a country named Syria about 1,000 miles from where Mom is in Qatar. Dad told me the leader of Syria was using bad chemicals on people, including children. We did see something on the news one Friday night about the USA and other countries trying to blow up the chemical storage buildings. It sounded like they hit the targets from what the news said. I guess it was the Air Force and the Navy that sent planes and bombs into Syria. I wondered why somebody like a leader would use chemicals on people, especially kids. I thought the leader must be really mean. I didn't think it was right.

Dad and I were super proud of Mom in situations like that. Dad said he was proud of her as an American, and he was proud to be her husband. It was crazy to think she was there and doing stuff like that to make some people's lives and the world better. I didn't know how to get my brain around it. She was there and supporting what is right.

A couple days later, Mom sent an email with some pictures and articles about what had happened there. In the first pictures, you could see the buildings where the chemicals were stored. In the later pictures, you couldn't. The bombings were so accurate in what they hit and what they didn't. There was also a picture of a B-1 bomber in the email. It was one of the new types of planes at Mom's base that she had been telling us about. They were replacing the older planes Mom had gotten me a bomb pin from. Dad said he had that picture on his computer screen at work. I asked him about it because I thought my picture was always on his computer at work. He said that since Mom had been away, my picture had been replaced. I wasn't sure how I felt about that…but I guess I was OK with it.

My piano recital was on a Monday night at my teacher's church. Nana and Papa came along with Dad and me. It was my third recital. The recitals usually go well. I hoped that night would be another good one. When we got to the church, I had to sit with the other students. That year I played "The Battle Hymn of the Republic" since Mom was away and in the service. I thought it would be a good song for the deployment. I'd been practicing it a lot. I had also practiced my introduction that I needed to say before I started playing. While I was waiting to perform, I would turn around and make faces at Dad when he was looking to laugh and relax a little.

When it was my turn, I introduced myself and sat down to begin playing. The first thing I noticed was that the keys were different on the piano there than on the one at my teacher's house or ours at home. I stopped and looked to my instructor for help. She came over right away. I was a little panicked, and I took a few deep breaths after she helped me to get aligned. Once I started playing, it went very well. Dad recorded it so we could show Mom on the phone later. When I got done with the song, I took a bow and sat back down with the other students.

I felt like I had really accomplished it! Mom and everyone said they were proud of me for how I played. That felt good! I'd been working on the song for about two months. I thought, "This may be the last time I play it since I will move on to new songs in my lessons."

Chapter 27

WEEKS 15 & 16:
THE FIGHT & BITE

About a week after the recital, something happened at school that upset me. There was this kid named Omir who sat next to me in class. Omir was born in Syria, then moved to Jordan and later moved here to the US. I had been helping him with reading, writing, and math. Some other kids helped him at times, but it was mostly me. We'd known each other since third grade. One day we were in art class and he was a little mad at me. He said, "Your mom is making our country worse and not doing anything good over there." I told the teacher on him and shared what Omir told me. She said she would feel bad also if her mom was deployed and protecting our country. It made me feel bad and angry with him because my mom was making our country and other parts of the world, like Syria, better.

When we got back to the classroom, our teacher started talking to him about what had happened. Omir told her that I was lying and making things up. At one point, she did pull both Omir and me together to talk about what happened.

Omir got to explain first, and then I got to tell my side. He told her I was lying about it. This had all happened at the art table, and I told her that two other kids also heard what he said to me. She called the other two kids over. They said they heard Omir saying this stuff to me. Then Omir started crying. Our teacher told us to go back and start packing up because it was the end of the day. I hoped that was the end of it. I still wanted to be friends with him, but I knew it might not be the same as it had been before. I was really hurt by what he said.

Mom received another package from Dad and me that week. We liked to send her magazines and her favorite snacks so she didn't miss out on the stuff she likes here at home. One thing she did say was that we could stop sending vitamins because she had enough to last her until she was done there. That just sounded funny to me at that point. But it also meant that the deployment was getting closer to being over.

On Saturday, we had our first Little League baseball game. That morning, I had told Dad I wasn't worried about getting hurt playing baseball because there's not as much contact as football. If the pitches got close to me, I could just move out of the way, kind of like dodgeball. We won over the Dodgers 17-7. It was so much fun! I liked all my teammates, and I felt it was a good teamwork lesson on how you need to stick together. I scored three runs and did good overall. Dad said he was proud of me, and that made me feel like I was on top of the world. I hoped the rest of the season would go like our first game. The next game would be on Thursday night.

On Sunday, the day after the game, Mom sent us a video of her working with a military dog. It was a German Shepherd. The video was crazy to watch. She was wearing protective gear on her upper body, the same thing dog trainers wear when they are teaching the dogs to attack bad people. The dog was barking a lot, and I could hear Mom saying in the video that she wasn't so sure she should be doing this, and some adult words! But after a little bit, the trainer let the dog loose near Mom and it went after her arm. I could hear the dog growling and Mom yelling, but she wasn't getting hurt—just being jerked around a lot. The dog never let go the entire time, which was about twenty or thirty seconds.

I thought it was neat that even with all the stuff going on over there, she had the chance to try things, even if it was getting attacked by a military dog. It showed me that sometimes when we aren't so sure about doing things because we're nervous or scared, we still need to go ahead and try. Kind of like baseball. I'm glad I tried that, too. It's fun.

On Monday, Dad and I went to see the counselor again. It was Dad's birthday, but we still went for about thirty minutes.

The biggest thing I talked about was the Omir situation at school. Miss Cynthia talked about trying to understand other people's thoughts and respecting them. I told her that I did understand and respect his thoughts, but I didn't think everything he said to me was fair or nice. She agreed.

Dad did most of the talking after that because Miss Cynthia was asking how things were going overall. I heard him say that he was proud of me and that most of the problems—if there were any—were, he thought, because I was a ten-year-old boy and not because Mom was away. He always asked that I just take care of myself and he would do the rest. The session went fast.

At school the next week, Omir and I got into a couple arguments again. One was over basketball when he was hitting me while we were playing. He wasn't punching me. It was just over-aggressive basketball playing. I was still hurt by what he had said about my mom, so it was difficult to be friends with him then.

Chapter 28

WEEK 17:
THE STRIKEOUT

I had done some online shopping for Dad's birthday with Nana, but the things we bought didn't get there in time. He'd been asking about them a lot. I told him he could open his presents when we went out for lunch with Nana and Papa after my next baseball game. We bought him a Brewers baseball cap and a Royals baseball cap. We got a Brewers one because that's his favorite baseball team and a Royals one because that was my baseball team's name. I wanted him to have a hat for my team too. He was scoring for all my games that year to help the coach. He wrote down every play and kept track of the other team too. He was busy, but I could still talk to him during the games because he was near the dugout where we sat.

On Tuesday, I got a package in the mail. It was a "sunshine package" from Aunt Lori. I thought it was nice of her to send me a package to help me feel better since my mom was gone. She knew I'd been sick a lot lately, too, and wanted to make me feel better. It had a bunch of snacks in it like crackers, peanut M&M's, and a bunch of items that were packaged in a yellow wrapper. I called to thank her for sending it to me right away. It definitely made me feel better then, and for a few more days after until all the snacks were gone. I was pretty sure she had also sent another package to my mom. Aunt Lori did a lot for her.

I had my second baseball game that week. We played the Orioles. There were three guys on that team that I knew from school. I was excited for the game, and also a little nervous since they were the best team in the league. Also, I was supposed to pitch an inning, which I obviously had never done before. The game was close, 8-4 going into the fifth inning with my team leading. Then, I was up to pitch. I told Dad in between innings I was a little worried about it. He said it was going to be OK no matter how I pitched. Everyone would understand because it was my first season.

When the first batter came up, I was SCARED. The first two pitches I threw were balls, but then I threw three strikes and got him out. I faced three more batters. One got a hit, but I struck out the other two to end the inning. We came to the dugout and everyone was cheering because we were out of time and the game was over. So, we won our second game 8-4 and our record was 2-0 for the year.

Dad said everyone had been cheering—my teammates, coaches, and family—but I didn't hear any of it when I was out on the mound. After the game, the coach had a quick meeting with all the players. He said he was proud of all of us. He said he was giving me the game ball because I put in the effort to help the team win by doing my job. That made me feel good about myself, but I was also a little bit shocked that I got the game ball. I felt like I had a huge smile on my face that I didn't want anyone to see. Dad, Nana, and Papa were all super proud of me. The other bonus was that I got to pick where we went for lunch, and I chose Burger King. After lunch, we went home to give Dad his birthday presents, which he'd been asking for all week. He really liked the hats I chose for him, along with the Brewers shirt from Nana. It seemed like everybody won that day! I just wished Mom had been there to share in all of it. Man, she missed out on so much. It wasn't fair.

Chapter 29

WEEK 18: EIGHT TIMES ZONES IN ONE DAY

Finally, May 12 was here! It was the day we had been planning for a while. It was time to go to Qatar and see Mom! We left from Chicago at dinnertime. We had to take two long flights. The first one was to Madrid, Spain. We flew through the night and arrived in the morning. We were there in time for breakfast. It was weird that we flew through all the time zones. The flight was about seven hours long, so getting there at breakfast time the next day was hard to understand until Dad explained time zones to me. He'd been to Europe three times, so he had some experience. On the flight there, I played on my phone and played *Battleship* on the TVs built into the backs of the seats. The airport in Spain was neat, but it was empty. We went to Starbucks for breakfast. While we were there, Mom called us. She wanted to see how we were doing in our travels. We didn't have a whole lot of time there before the next flight, which was the one to Qatar. It was pretty much breakfast and go. It was the same thing on that flight as it was on the flight to Spain. Phone time, some games like *Angry Birds*, and sleep. We got to Doha at dinnertime.

There had been food on the flights, but not a lot of what I liked to eat. Dad ate most of the food I didn't like and gave me the parts of his food that I liked. We had to go through customs in Doha, which was when I got the first stamp in my passport. They can look you up in their computer to make sure that you are who you say you are.

The airport in Doha was the best airport I have ever been in. It was really rich-looking and new. Dad said it was built four years ago. The people were nice, too. They helped us find things like the Baggage Area and Ground Transportation. From there, we took a taxi to our hotel. It was odd because of the type of cars everyone was driving. Most were Toyotas, VWs, or SUVs. Also, they were all the same color, white. Other cars we saw were Ferraris, BRZs, and Land Rovers. The cars the Qatari people drove were mostly white because it is always so hot there.

When we got to the hotel, it blew my mind out of the sea. Everything was fancy and rich-looking. It turns out that Qatar is the richest country in the world! Holy crap! No wonder everything was so nice there. We went up to our room, which was unbelievable. Dad got me my own bed. We hung out and watched TV. There were some English channels, but they were mostly showing movies. One thing that was good was that the Home and Garden channel was available for Mom.

Then, Monday finally came! It was the day we would see Mom for the first time since she had left. Dad and I got up and went to breakfast. I was excited to see Mom after four months! We walked around and checked out the hotel area. There were a lot of swimming pools and a beach area where we could go later if we wanted to. Then, after a little while, Mom called and said she was about fifteen minutes away from the hotel. We went down to the entrance to wait for her. I was nervous that Mom was going to show up in her military uniform. I wasn't sure what the Qataris would think if they saw her in it. I just never wanted her to get hurt or be in danger. Dad asked me why I was quiet, so I told him. He made me feel better by explaining that Qatar and the US are working together and the Qataris welcome the US military to their country. I wished he had told me that earlier because sometimes I just don't know that kind of stuff.

I saw an SUV pulling into the parking area and I saw Mom in the window. Dad didn't think it was her, but I was right. It was MOM! When she got out, I hugged her so tight that I thought I broke her ribs! Dad took a picture of us. After that, he hugged her really tight too. After all the hugging was done, the colonel came out of the SUV, and she was in her uniform. Mom introduced us to her. She seemed nice. She helped get some of Mom's stuff out and we shook hands with her. Then we went up to the hotel room. Mom liked the hotel, too. She couldn't believe how fancy it was.

Later that day, we went to the mall across the street to get some dinner. We went to a place called Sugar and Spice. They served hamburgers and other sandwiches, and some awesome desserts. We had a cake that had M&M's inside of it. It was the best cake I had ever had. Then we walked through the mall for a while. They have some of the same stores and restaurants we have here in the US, including McDonald's. After the mall, we went back to the hotel and chilled. Mom watched the Home and Garden channel. We went to bed kind of early since we were still adjusting to the time change.

Chapter 30

WEEK 18: CONTINUED...

The second day in Qatar was Tuesday. We went to a place called Banana Island. Mom had heard from some people that this was a nice place for a family to hang for a day. Even though it was really hot, we were on a beach or in swimming pools all day. I was glad Mom had us go to a place like this because I don't know what we'd have done if she didn't. Maybe stay at the hotel all day, I guess.

We took a taxi to the place where we got on a ferry. The ferry then took us to the island. It was kind of neat because it was air-conditioned on the inside the ferry, and it had TVs. It was about a thirty-minute ride to the island. It looked like it was a man-made island because it had island huts and stone buildings. Some buildings you could tell were more regular, like the entertainment building and restaurants. We went to the main building to get a map and learn what was all there. After that, we went to the beach and found some chairs and a cabana to lay out and relax in. It had to be awesome for Mom to be able to finally relax. After doing Air Force stuff for the last four months, this had to feel good. I was glad I was there with her and Dad.

There was a lot to do. The swimming pools were awesome. They had three slides going into one pool. We all went down a few times. We even raced using a phone stopwatch to see who was the fastest. There were three speeds of slides, and one was really long. On the beach was this big swing that was over the water. It was right at the edge. You had to walk in the water a little, then jump onto it.

The temperature was over 95 degrees but swinging made it feel cooler. Mom and I each took turns on the swing while Dad took pictures of us.

After a while, we went for lunch at this place called Ted's American Food. You could get regular cheeseburgers, sodas, and fries. It was kind of like being back home with the way it was decorated. The food was good, plus we got a peanut butter shake. It may have been the best shake I have ever had. We were sharing the shake, but I think I had more than anyone else.

From there, we went to the entertainment building, where there were some bowling lanes. We played one game of island bowling. Island bowling is where you bowl barefoot if you want to. Dad won, and I just barely beat Mom. After that, Mom and I played against Dad in tennis on one of the tennis courts they had. It was cool because we could see the gulf from there. It looked like a picture.

After tennis, we had to head back to the main building to catch the ferry back to Doha. The air-conditioning felt good again, just like it had on the way to the island.

When we got back to Doha, Mom planned for us to go to the Islamic Museum. The building on the outside was beautiful. It looked old and new at the same time. We got to see some ancient tools and weapons. I couldn't believe how old some of the stuff was. There were items that were over a thousand years old. We didn't go through the entire museum because it was getting late, but what we did see was pretty cool. We did go outside on a deck of the museum to look around. We could see downtown Doha and all the buildings in the skyline. Many were still being built. It was dark when we got back to the hotel. We basically relaxed the rest of the night in our room. It felt good just to hang out as a family again.

On Wednesday, we took a desert safari. This was the next thing Mom planned for all of us to do. Right after breakfast, we got picked up at our hotel by a man named King Amir. He was dressed in all-white traditional clothing for men. From there, he took us out of the city and into the desert, which took about an hour. On the drive, we saw some exotic cars, a real neat soccer stadium, and lots of buildings and roads being built. King Amir told us that they need to build seven more soccer stadiums because Qatar would be hosting the World Cup in four years. We also saw the mall that we would be going to on Thursday.

King Amir was a cool guy and such a nice man. He was also the president of the company, Falcon Tours. He told us so much while he was driving. It was like going to school in Qatar. He told us that he was from Pakistan and his family was still there. He came to Doha to start his business. He gave us a lot of information about the soccer stadiums and how the city of Doha had basically been built in the last ten years. He pretty much talked and answered his phone all the way there.

When we got to the place where his company was located, there was nothing but sand dunes everywhere. It was the real desert, like you see in books. We also saw some camels that had harnesses and stuff on them so you could ride them. There were cell towers out there for the 4G network. It just seemed funny to have cell towers and nothing else. The camels were crazy, not something I ever expected see up close in real life or thought I'd be able to ride.

It was odd how the camels knelt for us to get on them. Once we climbed on and the camels started to get up, it felt like we were going to fall forward until they were on all four feet. The person who was with the camels, one of King Amir's workers, then walked us for a while with all three of us on our own camels. It was kind of a bumpy ride because of how they walked. The worker also took pictures of us in a few spots.

When we got back about twenty minutes later, he took us to a tent that had old couches for us to sit on. He gave Mom and Dad some tea that the local people drink. They said they liked it, but I didn't want to try it. While we were resting, he let us hold his pet falcon on our arms. We had to wear the trainer's glove, and the falcon was leashed so he couldn't fly away. The man took pictures of us while King Amir was on the phone. He seemed like a busy person. The falcon did spread his wings while he was on Mom's arm, so you could see just how long his wings were. After we took some pictures, it was time to get into the truck to go out onto the sand dunes.

It really felt and looked like we were on the other side of the world. There was nothing but sand everywhere. King Amir was our driver, and he drove really crazy! He went fast and slow, up and down the sand dunes. Sometimes he even went sideways on the dunes and it felt like we were going to tip over and roll down the hill. He would stop at the top of a dune and literally let the truck slide down the hill until we reached the bottom. Then he would take off really fast again. The one time he really freaked me out was when he was going to stop so we could take a picture. Then he pretended like something was wrong and we actually slid down the sand dune backwards! It was scary and crazy. We were all laughing so hard and not believing it at the same time. It felt good to see Mom laughing, screaming, and having fun. All of us were really enjoying it. I was so happy for her after everything she'd had to deal with during deployment.

When we were out really far into the dunes, King Amir took us to a place for pictures. We stood at the edge of Qatar and the Persian Gulf and saw Saudi Arabia across the water. Those were some neat pictures. We also went looking for rocks for our next-door neighbor, Erin. She asked that we bring back some special rocks from Qatar for her niece and nephew. Erin was taking care of Bear while we were gone, so I was glad to do it. After we found some cool rocks and took pictures, we started to head back to the camp where we started from. It seemed like a longer ride back. From there, it was back to the hotel.

After some rest at the hotel, we got into a taxi and went to the *souq*, or street market. My mom heard about that place and had been there once before. When we first arrived, it looked like a scene out of a movie. The buildings seemed really old.

Like a hundred years old. But Mom said that all the buildings had been built in the last few years and were made to look that way. It was done to show respect and have an understanding of what it looked like a long time ago. The first thing we did was take a picture of where the taxi dropped us off, just in case we got lost. It wasn't very crowded at first since the souq was just opening. We walked around for a while and went into some of the stores as they opened. One of them we walked into was an old-school candy store with all kinds of candy inside. Most of it was candy we could buy in America, but there were also big bowls of candy where you could buy one piece at a time. It was different kinds of hard candy. We decided to all try a piece or two. One of the kinds I had tasted like sour green apple.

We kept walking around and saw more of the buildings. We bought some souvenirs for people back home who had been helping us. Mom bought some little jewelry boxes and bracelets as thank-you gifts. Dad found me a neat Qatar soccer shirt and shorts, and he bought a Qatar World Cup T-shirt for himself. Mom bought some shoes.

While we were shopping, I found some kittens. I got to play with them for a while, which was fun. We don't have kittens running around stores back home. If we did, I might want to shop more with Mom. Besides the kittens, we found a whole pet animal area where there were more cats, dogs, turtles, rabbits, and lots of birds, big and small. It was REALLY noisy. I don't think I could ever have a bird as a pet.

The temperature was so hot. I think it was close to 100 degrees. We decided to look for someplace to eat and get a drink. We had seen a pizza place earlier as we walked around, but Mom and Dad couldn't remember where we'd seen it. I kind of remembered the way, so I told them to trust me. We walked in the direction where I thought it was, and we found it. I have always been good at directions. It was decorated like an Italian restaurant we'd see back home. We ordered some waters, sodas, and a pizza. For some reason, the pizza tasted like the best pizza we ever had. It seemed weird having such a good pizza in a place like that, or should I say, in Qatar. Even though it was a long day, it was nice to be able to relax and talk about everything we had done in the desert. I started to think about how this day was Wednesday, which meant we had only one more day together before Dad and I had to go home.

I have to say, I never felt unsafe in that country. Even with Mom being at an Air Force base forty miles from Doha, I felt safe. The people were nice and friendly. Dad seemed to really enjoy the culture and time with Mom. My family was so happy just to be together. I realized how lucky I was as a ten-year-old kid to be able to do that stuff.

Chapter 31

THE LAST DAY IN DOHA

On our last day in Qatar, we went to the Villaggio Mall. We took another taxi there. Taxis were always ready and waiting for us at the hotel. One thing that was special about our last day was that it was also the start of Ramadan. I really didn't know much about this holiday, so Mom and Dad explained a lot of it to me. What was very odd to me was that you couldn't eat or drink for the entire day, from sunrise to sunset. Mom and Dad couldn't kiss or hold hands, either. That day was the beginning of it, and it lasted for thirty days. We asked taxi drivers and they all said they honored it. Most said that it wasn't that hard to go all day without eating or drinking. I am not sure I could do it.

Once we got to the mall, it was unlike any mall I had ever seen. It was not crowded because of Ramadan. We could walk around easily. It had a ceiling that was painted like the sky with clouds. It looked real. In the middle of the mall, you could go on a boat ride like they have in Italy. Mom said it was called a gondola. All of us got in it and there was a man dressed like he was in Italy driving and steering the boat. It took us all the way to the other end and then back to where we started. We saw the amusement area where they had the rides that we'd go on later.

We walked through the mall for a while and then finally got to the ride area. The first one we went on was the go-karts, like we have back home. They were fast. It was cool that something like this was here for people to do. I didn't think that it would be so much like the US. We had the track to ourselves. I won, Mom was second, and Dad was third, or last. He did bump into me to let me know he was there, but he couldn't pass me, and then Mom passed him right at the end. We took driving seriously.

There were other rides, like a zip line ride we each went on. We'd done this in Florida several times, but in Qatar, we went on a track instead of a cable. There was also a roller coaster, which was pretty fun, too. There were also lots of arcade games we played while Dad went shopping. Mom wanted Dad to find something special from Qatar since she was missing his birthday and Father's Day. All the restaurants were closed because of Ramadan. It was our last day as a family, but we did what we always do. We had lots of fun!

Once we got back to the hotel, Mom and Dad went for massages. I had a chance to chill for an hour while they were gone. I was able to use my phone for the first time since being in Qatar. It was still weird to me that we could do so much here just like we could back home. I just thought that there was nothing in Qatar, but now that I have been there, I've learned differently. I was glad that my mom could get a massage and relax before she went back to the Air Force base tomorrow. We had a lot of fun that week! I had a warm feeling inside when we were together.

Once Mom and Dad got back, we went down to the restaurant to have some dinner. All the blinds were closed for

Ramadan until sunset. There were some other people eating. We waited as long as we could until sunset when we could eat again. More pizza! I think Mom and Dad did it for me. The had a big screen TV that the movie *Despicable Me* was playing on. It was one more time where I thought that it still felt like America. We talk about our favorite things all the time. We also have a rule that we cannot repeat each other. My favorite part was the desert safari, Mom's was the Villaggio Mall where we did all the rides, and Dad's was Banana Island.

Later that night, we started packing. Dad and I had to fly back home in the morning. I wasn't ready to go home yet, especially knowing that we would be leaving Mom back here. In the morning, we had to get up early and take a taxi for the last time to go to the airport. Leaving Mom was sad, but not as sad as the first time she left. I knew the time was getting closer for her to come home, so it made me stronger. She stayed at the hotel after we left because she did not have to be back at the base until the end of the day. When we got to the airport, we got some breakfast and waited for our first flight to London, then Chicago. We would finish up with the drive home. It was another long day of travel, but it was all worth it for our family time!

Chapter 32

WEEK 19: LOOKING BACK

On the flight back, Dad and I were talking about the whole deployment. I remembered when Mom and Dad first told me about it. I was thinking back to the things I was concerned about at that time:

- Are you going to war?
- Are you going to die?
- Do you get guns?
- When will it start?
- Who will do everything that you do, Mom?

Our trip was towards the end of deployment, and I think most of my questions had been answered. There really wasn't that much to worry about. Things had a way of working out. My family had really worked as a team to get stuff done, and that was the most important thing. Mom did go to war, but she was working at an Air Force base where she was seeing and planning bombings. She didn't die. She did get to have guns if she needed them, and Dad had been taking care of everything Mom would normally do. Dad always said to take care of myself and he would take care of the rest, and that is exactly what had happened. He did have to remind me, though. I knew he'd been really busy managing everything. Mom said I should make a thank-you note for him. Sometimes it was hard to believe that it would work out, but it did. We talked to Mom almost every day, so we all knew what was going on and when things were happening. Mom even knew about Little League and wished me good luck before every game. Traveling back home gave Dad and I time to really talk about all this stuff. We realized that we have such a strong family and we helped each other through all of this. The plane rides went well, and we stayed on schedule.

The day after we got back from Qatar, I had a baseball game at 8:30 in the morning. I woke up early and was ready to play. Dad was already up and doing laundry. It was beginning to feel like a normal Saturday, not a day where we had traveled halfway around the world the day before. My life was crazy.

The game was fun, but we lost. I asked Dad if Ethan could come over to play later and he said it was fine. He contacted Ethan's parents to arrange a time. That made it feel even more like a normal Saturday. By the end of the day, I had fallen asleep early on the couch and didn't even know Mom called until Dad woke me for a minute to say "hi." Mom was back on the base and Dad and I were back home. Silly to think we had just been together on the other side of the world the day before. Part of me wished I was still there, but another part just wished Mom was back home.

I did what Mom asked and made Dad a thank-you note. I left it under his pillow so he would find it when he went to bed. Dad was so happy. Like usual, he cried. It must have meant a lot to him.

Chapter 33

WEEKS 20-24: SCHOOLS OUT...SHOW ME THE MONEY!

Monday came, and it was back to school. I only had a couple weeks left before I would be done with fourth grade. It had been my favorite year so far because of the challenges I'd had overcome. The biggest was Mom being gone, but there were others, too. I hadn't been sure how I was going to do in school because I was worrying about Mom at the start of the year. I thought I was going to do bad at everything because I was so sad. It turned out that I did great. Dad said my tests had been good, and I kept my grades where they needed to be. I also went up three levels in reading, which was my goal at the beginning of the year. Math was still my favorite, and that had gone pretty well, too. I wouldn't miss the homework when the year ended, though. Plus, with all the rainouts we'd had for baseball, I'd be playing a lot of games in June, so that was something to look forward to after school was done.

Memorial Day weekend arrived. We had no school on Friday or Tuesday, so we had five days off in a row. And after that, there were only eight days of school left. Memorial Day weekend was always fun because we put out a bunch of US flags along the driveway and sidewalk until Monday night. Mom and I had always done it in the past, so Dad filled in that year. He also lowered the flag on Monday, Memorial Day, to remember all the soldiers. Sundays are Dad's favorite day of the week—and mine, kind of—because of all the races on TV that we like to watch. The Indianapolis 500 and the NASCAR races always do special things to remember the soldiers. For NASCAR, they even paint red, white, and blue onto the cars somehow to help celebrate. It meant so much more that year with what Mom was going through.

I found myself journaling less and less at the end of the school year. Maybe it was because I felt better after seeing my mom in Qatar and knowing that we were getting closer to her return. I was not as sad anymore. I felt like everything was looking up. Mom was coming home soon, school was ending, and I had nothing but the summer ahead of me.

We had been back from our trip to Qatar and seeing Mom for about three weeks when school ended. There was only one half-day left. We didn't do much that day, just got our yearbooks and went to the gym so we could sign them. The kids didn't write much, mostly just their names. Usually Mom and Dad would both be there at pick-up for my last day. Mom would make one of her signs with my name on it and something about the last day, like "You Did It!" It was only Dad this year. I felt sad about that, but we had gotten used to it by then. I got to pick where I wanted to go for lunch. Burger King was my favorite, so when Dad asked, that's what I said. After lunch, we headed home. I got to play Xbox with some of my friends that were online. I played for almost two hours, which was a treat.

Dad talked to me later and said that he and Mom were trying to figure out what my graduation present would be. They'd been talking about giving me a hundred dollars for each year of school. So, that year I would get $400. I would need to deposit $300 into my bank account and would get to keep $100 for myself to use on anything. I was hyped! There was only one thing I was going to spend it on, and that was *Fortnite* stuff. It would allow me to get more tiers and items from the store. Some of the stuff looked really cool. That was an awesome present. $100 dollars for every year! I couldn't wait till I was in the twelfth grade!

Chapter 34

THE FINISH LINE

Since summer had arrived, I'd been busy playing with friends and enjoying my time. Most of the calls from Mom had been talking about when she thought she would be able to leave. It sounded like she would not know for sure until just a few days before. Her travel back would take a lot longer than ours did because she had to fly with the military. She didn't sound excited about that at all.

A few days before her return, Dad and I texted everyone about Mom coming home. I was getting so excited because I was going to have my whole family back together again. Mom only wanted to have the family at the airport because she didn't want it to be a big deal. She was going to be traveling for over thirty-two hours, so she was going to be tired. Most of the family said they would come. We finally knew that it was going to be Sunday, July 15. I know I will never forget that day.

Dad and I picked up flowers and we made signs for Mom. Aunt Lori also made a finish line out of a roll of toilet paper so that Mom and I could run through it. I was feeling excited as we drove to the airport. When Dad and I arrived, we saw

Uncle Tom, Aunt Lori, and Nana and Papa. Everyone else showed up after us. (Aunt Sue, Uncle John, Aunt Cyndee, Uncle Bob, some people from my mom's base, et cetera.) We were all talking with each other and looking to see if we could see her.

When my mom was walking down the jetway with another Air Force soldier, it was so amazing to see her again. I ran to her and she hugged me first. We met in the middle of the finish line. The hug felt amazing, and I was so excited that I was finishing this chapter in my life. I had wanted this chapter behind me so badly. Mom hugged everyone else and we talked for a little bit. We also took a few pictures. It was over!

We headed home after the airport so Mom could see a few surprises that Dad and I had for her. Dad had a TV installed in the garage, which is what Mom always wanted. We love being outside in the summer, and now we could watch TV out there, too. We also had flags and balloons around the yard. Mom was so happy. She acted like she had just seen a quadruple rainbow or something. I had never seen my mom that happy.

The first thing we did was take turns smashing Mom's watch with a hammer. It was a cheap watch she had bought for the deployment, so we wanted to smash it to symbolize the end of our time apart. I took the first hit and Mom finished it off. It felt pretty good to hit something like that. After it was smashed, I threw it into the pond. That was one of the best moments of my life. Next, my mom took out the green light that we had lit since she left. That light was on continuously as a symbol of us thinking of her. We had so many family members and friends who lit green lights for my mom. It was neat to finally shut it off and get rid of the green light.

That was a night I will never forget. I had happy tears several times because my mom was home. It felt like my world was balanced again. It felt like a weight had been lifted off my shoulders. The weight had been pretty heavy for a ten-year-old to carry around. I will always remember what I went through. Having my mom gone for that long and having her doing military things had been hard for me, but once she was home, it started to feel pretty cool because it was behind us.

As I thought back about the six and a half months when she was away, I realized the deployment had been a big learning experience. I would tell other kids that if they have to go through this with one of their parents, it will all be OK. It is worth it when you get your mom back and you hug for the first time. You need to be strong as a family, and if you do that, you will get through it. Each of us did our part and the green light had been shining through it all.

Epilogue

My mom has been home now about the same amount of time that she was deployed. Since she got back, she has been quieter and less talkative than she was before she left. I felt bad for her because I just wanted my mom to be back to normal. Although it took her awhile to adjust, she is finally getting better.

Mom got to see me play baseball for the first time and was excited that I was doing so good at something new. Once baseball ended, the indoor football season started and Mom made it to every game.

It feels so good in my house again because everything is settling down. Mom and Dad are back into a routine with tasks around the house and we have more time for fun, just like Dad said we would. I feel like I even sleep better at night because Mom is closer to me.

I started my final year of elementary school with Mom and Dad by my side. I have been doing better with school and I haven't been as sick as I was when she was gone. When everything is back in balance in my life, things go better.

Mom has gone to a few sessions out at her base to help her adjust back into her daily life. It seems like it's helped her. She doesn't like taking the time away from Dad and me to go, but in the end it's worth it. She said that the adjustment back to her everyday life has been harder than she thought it was going to be.

We have gone to see Miss Cynthia and she continues to help us talk through the changes in our family. My mom has said a few times that she feels different, maybe she always will.

As I worked to finish this book, Mom has shared this experience with so many people. She is proud of me, and it seems like everyone she talks to is impressed that I wrote this book to help other kids. She has met so many people with military connections including a guy who started an organization where he connects dogs with veterans. It's called Dogs2DogTags. This organization is special because they donated towards the publishing costs of this book. In return, I am donating some of the proceeds back to them. These dogs help veterans feel better. My hope is that someday my book will help other kids feel better too.

I want to give a special thanks to my mom, dad, Aunt Lori and Miss Cynthia. Without their help and support this book would have never happened.

Dogs2DogTags.org

43198021R00087

Made in the USA
Lexington, KY
25 June 2019